HOW TO
CAST OUT
DEMONS

ISAIAH SALDIVAR

HOW TO
CAST
OUT
DEMONS

CHARISMA
HOUSE

Cataloging-in-Publication Data is on file with the Library of Congress.
International Standard Book Number: 978-1-63641-415-7
E-book ISBN: 978-1-63641-416-4

2 2024
Printed in the United States of America

Most Charisma Media products are available at special quantity discounts for bulk purchase for sales promotions, premiums, fundraising, and educational needs. For details, call us at (407) 333-0600 or visit our website at www.charismamedia.com.

This book is dedicated to my Nino Ben, who never stopped believing in me. Thank you for tirelessly serving, mentoring, and being a spiritual father to me since day one. If it were not for you, I genuinely do not believe I would be where I am today and would not have been able to write this book. You're a legend.

CONTENTS

FOREWORD

I'M NOT ON social media like my friends Isaiah Saldivar and Vladimir Savchuk, but I joke with them by saying Vlad is better looking. Actually, it is a tie. They are both great men of God.

In my book *When Pigs Move In*, I say we should be raising up armies instead of audiences. I believe that is happening today, and Isaiah is one of the leaders. He is right when he says there is an army rising up, a mighty remnant that is casting out demons, laying hands on the sick, and seeing miracles happen. There's a mighty move of God underway, and in this book, Isaiah shows how you can be part of it.

As you begin this journey through the pages of *How to Cast Out Demons*, may you be equipped, empowered, and emboldened to stand firm in the face of spiritual opposition. May you discover afresh the reality of Christ's victory over the powers of darkness and walk in the freedom and authority that He has secured for you.

It is my prayer that this book will serve as a beacon of light in a world shrouded in darkness, guiding believers to greater depths of spiritual understanding, intimacy with God, and victory in spiritual warfare.

—DON DICKERMAN
FOUNDER, DON DICKERMAN MINISTRIES
AND LIBERATED LIVING
AUTHOR OF *WHEN PIGS MOVE IN*; *KEEP THE PIGS OUT*;
PEOPLE, PIGS, AND PRINCIPALITIES;
AND *PROTECTED BY ANGELS*

Chapter 1
THEY SHALL CAST OUT DEMONS

I T'S JANUARY 12, 2011, and I'm about to go to church for the first time in three years. Although I was raised in a godly, Christian home and homeschooled my entire life, at sixteen I graduated high school, got a job, and decided I would no longer believe in God or attend church. Instead, I would become an atheist.

Fast-forward three years: Now nineteen years old and soon to graduate college, I was ready to pursue my dream job and become a deputy sheriff in California. So far everything seemed to be going as planned. The only reason I agreed to go to church that night was that for months my little sister had been begging me to go. She said, "Just go one time, and I'll stop asking you."

I told my girlfriend, "Let's go one time just to shut her up." I truly had no intention of ever going to church again after that night. Little did I know my entire world was about to be flipped upside down.

I remember vividly, as I stepped through the door of the church, telling myself, "This will be the last time I ever do this." In all her pleading my sister had said, "Isaiah, at this church you will feel God." This was bizarre to me, as up until this point I had never "felt God." I do recall, though, feeling something odd when I stepped into that church. The only way I could describe it was feeling as if there was a presence in the room. I now know this was God, but at the time I was clueless.

I sat in the back of this very large church, thinking I was just going to get this over with. I didn't want to talk to anyone, engage in any activities, or even be noticed. I just wanted to get in and get out and get this over with. The preacher began to talk about world missions and how many people were unreached for Christ. When he was ready to make the altar call, he said something that struck me: "Do you want to be next year in the same place you are this year?" I thought about how stagnant my life was, how each year I was partying with the same people, doing the same things, as if my life was just going in circles. Often I would lie in bed at night staring at the ceiling, thinking there had to be more to life than this.

The pastor gave the altar call and said, "If you're ready for change, if you want God in your life, come up here!"

My heart began to race, and I felt something—or should I say someone—pulling on my shirt. It was so intense I got out of my chair, stepped over my girlfriend and a friend I was with, and rushed down to the altar, thinking, "What is happening? What am I doing?" I did not know at the time that the Bible says in John 6:44 that nobody comes to the Father unless the Spirit draws him. I was like a fish being violently reeled in by a fisherman; I couldn't deny it or even fight it. Here I was at the altar, having no clue what to do or say, and all that came out of my mouth was, "God, I don't believe in You!" I actually used profanity. "But if You're real, I'll give You everything. I'll break up with my girlfriend of four years. If You're real, I'll leave the career I'm pursuing in law enforcement. If You're real, show me! I'll do anything!"

Although I claimed to be an atheist, I was desperate for God. I was so desperate to know there was more to life than just partying, pursuing a career, and having "stuff." The moment those words left my mouth, an audible voice spoke from the sky—not an inward whisper, not a still, small voice, but a loud voice from above said, "Isaiah, I don't want 99 percent of you. If you give Me everything, I will use you." I was in complete shock because not only did I realize God was real, but He knew *my name.* The God of the universe was calling me by name.

> I was like a fish being violently reeled in by a fisherman. All that came out of my mouth was, "God, I don't believe in You! But if You're real, I'll give You everything."

By now I was experiencing some out-of-body vision with a bright light in front of me and around me. God showed me everything He was going to use me to do, and I saw myself on a stage preaching to thousands of people. In so many words, He said, "Isaiah, I want to use you to preach the gospel to the nations." I responded, "I have nothing to offer You; I don't know any pastors, I don't know the Bible, I am unholy, I have a filthy mouth, and I live a filthy lifestyle." To that God replied, "I'll take your hands, I'll take your feet, I'll take your mouth, and I will use you."

In a moment I felt as if I was back in my body, and when I

came to, I was speaking in tongues. Mind you, I had heard this only one time in my entire life as a young kid. I tried to cover my mouth because now my girlfriend was standing next to me at the altar, but the tongues wouldn't stop—they gushed out of me. I bawled like a baby (I hadn't cried in ten years because my heart was so hard), and the next thing that happened still baffles me to this day: Literal dirt started coming out of my eyes. As this was happening, the pastor got on stage and said, "There is a young man here, and God says He is removing the dirty scales from your eyes!" Keep in mind there were several hundred people at the altar.

Finally, I said, "Lord, what do You want from me? What do I do?" He responded, "Pray one hour a day, and I'll show you." The moment the Lord spoke that to me, the pastor said, "God is calling some of you to pray one hour a day." With the pastor confirming everything God spoke, I couldn't deny this even if I wanted to. That night, I was born again; I repented of my sin and put my faith in the finished work of the cross. I went from death to life, and years of anger, depression, anxiety, lust, bitterness, and addiction were broken by the power of the Holy Spirit.

"SOMETHING HAPPENED TO ISAIAH!"

So radical was this transformation that I didn't sleep for three full days or eat for almost two weeks. Day and night I prayed and witnessed to friends and family.

I remember going home and getting rid of all my ungodly music, movies, and video games, and pretty much anything in my life that didn't have to do with God. I immediately knew I would not be in law enforcement but would spend the rest of my life preaching the gospel. My family called my uncle Ben, or Nino (it means godfather), who had been in ministry for over thirty years. He was doing a conference in New York, and they said, "You need to get home fast! Something happened to Isaiah!"

When my nino got home, for ten or twelve hours straight I told him everything God was showing me. I said, "Nino, God showed me a revival breaking out at my house and all my friends and family getting saved!" He said, "OK, so what is God saying to do?" And I said, "Pray!" (I'm skipping many details, but someday I will write an entire book about what God did in my living room.)

So we began to pray. It started with only a few of us in my living room, and within a matter of three or four months up to five hundred people were gathering every single week at my house. (We had a big country property.) People would be outside looking through the windows to hear what God was doing, and miracles, signs, and wonders were breaking out daily. We ended up naming this The Awakening 209 (209 was our area code).

That revival lasted ten years, and during it I traveled with my nino over one hundred thousand miles a year all throughout the United States, preaching in about five hundred churches. Countless miracles took place during this revival: blind eyes opening, deaf ears being healed, families being restored, people being healed of incurable diseases, and demons being cast out.

You might be curious why I'm sharing this entire testimony in a book titled *How to Cast Out Demons*, and the reason is it was there in my living room that I learned about deliverance. It was there I began to see my old party friends and family members come in, and as we prayed, they would start manifesting demons, and we would cast them out. It's not like I learned about deliverance and then did it; this was on-the-job training. We were learning as it was happening. For the next decade I would cast out demons any chance I got and share about the freedom we have in Christ.

By late 2020 my online ministry had taken off. We were

5

reaching millions of people a month and gained close to a million followers in one year, when suddenly I had an experience with the Holy Spirit that changed the trajectory of my ministry. Up until this time, I had preached about deliverance ministry once in a while but never more than a few minutes in a sermon.

> There is a war going on in the heavenly realms, and if you don't fight, who will? It is time to get off the sidelines and get on the front lines.

I was casting out demons from 2011–2020, but it was never an emphasis of my ministry.

Then one night as I was in prayer, the Holy Spirit told me in so many words, "Isaiah, I want you to train My church to cast out demons; they are unequipped and unprepared for the war that is coming. Will you take on this assignment?" He made me aware that there would be a cost; I would be ridiculed, talked about, and bad-mouthed for doing this ministry. I said yes, I would do it—thinking this would be a one-week teaching on how to cast out demons on my live stream. What I didn't realize was that for the next six months, every single week, I would teach about casting out demons. These videos would get millions of views, and God truly birthed a deliverance movement during that season.

I am convinced that God is calling every Christian to cast out demons. There is a war going on in the heavenly realms, and if you don't fight, who will? If you don't go, who will? It is time to get off the sidelines and get on the front lines; it is time to get off the cruise ship and get on the battleship; it is time to come out of the stands and get on the field. The people around you depend on you to help them get free.

THREE COMMISSIONS

Jesus gave three main commissions when it came to casting out demons.

The first commission is in Matthew 10:5–8 when He calls His twelve disciples to cast out demons. It reads:

> Jesus sent out the twelve apostles with these instructions: "Don't go to the Gentiles or the Samaritans, but only to the people of Israel—God's lost sheep. Go and announce to them that the Kingdom of Heaven is near. Heal the sick, raise the dead, cure those with leprosy, and cast out demons. Give as freely as you have received!"

Notice that He did not ask them to do this; He told them to. This was a command from our Lord to these twelve disciples. Sometimes as believers we think we can pick and choose what we obey, but clearly Jesus was serious about this ministry, as all twelve of His disciples were called to do it. Now, you might be thinking, "Isaiah, I'm not one of the twelve apostles. This doesn't apply to me!" Let's keep going.

The second commission is in Luke 10:17–20 (NIV), where Jesus sends out the seventy-two disciples, and they return saying:

> "Lord, even the demons submit to us in your name." He replied, "I saw Satan fall like lightning from heaven. I have given you authority to trample on snakes and scorpions and to overcome all the power of the enemy; nothing will harm you. However, do not rejoice that the spirits submit to you, but rejoice that your names are written in heaven."

Now, remember, these were not the twelve apostles. These were seventy-two disciples, and Jesus said, "I have given you authority to trample on snakes and scorpions and to overcome all the power of the enemy." Jesus is obviously not speaking of actual snakes and scorpions here but of unclean spirits. You still might say, "But Isaiah, this doesn't apply to me! I'm not one of the seventy-two disciples." Let's keep going.

The third commission now applies to every believer. If you're a believer, this is for you. Mark 16:15–18 says:

> And then he told them, "Go into all the world and preach the Good News to everyone. Anyone who believes and is baptized will be saved. But anyone who refuses to believe will be condemned. These miraculous signs will accompany those who believe: They will cast out demons in my name, and they will speak in new languages. They will be able to handle snakes with safety, and if they drink anything poisonous, it won't hurt them. They will be able to place their hands on the sick, and they will be healed."

How incredible is this! The first sign of a believer is that they will cast out demons; not they might, not they can, but they *will*! Another important point is that we do not follow signs and wonders, but the signs and wonders follow us. There should be a trail of signs and wonders behind us if we truly believe. The world does not need another definition of Christianity. They need a demonstration of Christianity. To me the text is clear: This is for every believer.

Some people overlook what verse 20 in Mark 16 says: "And they went out and preached everywhere, the Lord working with them and confirming the word through the accompanying signs" (NKJV). The Lord continues to work with those who believe, confirming His Word with signs, healings, and miracles. When you cast out demons and pray for the sick, two significant things happen: God *confirms* the word you preach and *works* with you. This is incredible. As Mark says, the Lord suddenly starts working with us when we cast out demons. If you ever wanted to know how to get God to work with you, cast out demons. Don't believe the religious lie that God will deliver someone only if He wants to. No; He wants to partner with you to cast out demons. You must participate in this divine partnership.

In John 14:12 Jesus says, "I tell you the truth, anyone who believes in me will do the same works I have done, and even greater works because I am going to be with the Father." One of the main works Jesus did was casting out demons. Mark 1:39 says, "So he traveled throughout the region of Galilee, preaching in the synagogues and casting out demons."

It could not be clearer: If Jesus did it, we will also do it. Some may think that casting out demons is a special calling or spiritual gift, but if you look through the different church offices (Eph. 4:11) and the spiritual gifts (1 Cor. 12), you will notice deliverance is not there. That's because it's not a church office or a spiritual gift; it's the call of every believer! The devil has lied to us for so long that this is only for a select few superanointed people, but this couldn't be any further from the truth.

Think about it in the most basic sense: If I am a Christian, that means I am a follower of Christ, someone who lives like Christ on earth. If Christ healed the sick and cast out demons, and I am an ambassador according to 2 Corinthians 5:20 (NIV), which says, "We are therefore Christ's ambassadors, as though God were making his appeal through us," wouldn't it be logical to say that I am supposed to be setting people free? To say I shouldn't be doing this is to say I shouldn't do what Christ did. Christ was the model for the life we have been called to live. An ambassador is a representative sent by one country to another, authorized to speak and act on behalf of their home country. As Christ's ambassadors we are authorized to speak and act on His behalf, bringing His message of healing and freedom to those around us.

It saddens me how many Christians are OK with their friends and family being demonized and choose to do nothing about it. When are you going to get tired of seeing everyone around you in bondage while you have the answer? The Bible says in Romans 8:11, "The Spirit of God, who raised Jesus from the dead, lives in you. And just as God raised Christ Jesus from the dead, he will give life to your mortal bodies by this same Spirit living within you." You do not have a junior Holy Spirit; you do not have a weak, lesser version of the Holy Spirit; you have the *same* Spirit that raised Christ inside you! It's time to go to war against the forces of darkness that keep our friends and families in bondage. If we are going to fight against these unclean spirits, it's important we know a little more about them.

What Is a Demon?

In the simplest terms a demon is a person without a body. These beings do not have physical forms, so they seek to inhabit bodies. Demons crave a body to live in so they can carry out their evil actions. Paul describes the function of Satan's kingdom in Ephesians 6:12 (NKJV): "For we do not wrestle against flesh and blood, but against principalities, against powers, against the rulers of the darkness of this age, against spiritual hosts of wickedness in the heavenly places." International Bible teacher and deliverance minister Derek Prince, who studied Greek for over fifty years, explains it like this: "For our wrestling match is not against persons with bodies."[1] *The Living Bible* describes demons as "persons without bodies."

So Paul is saying that in the kingdom of darkness we are engaged in a wrestling match with beings that do not have physical bodies. They're not human, but they are still persons—just without bodies. This is why, in teaching spiritual warfare, we focus on the names and actions of demons. They have personalities: They get angry, they get sad, they cry, they laugh, and they have emotions. They are just like humans but without flesh and blood. We must also remember they have been around for thousands of years and are much smarter than we are.

I was casting a demon out of someone once, and it was extremely stubborn and would not leave. In a desperate attempt to get it out—and because I had tried everything else—I began to preach about the cross to it. I talked about how Jesus carried His cross to Golgotha, died for our sins, and defeated Satan. I was going on and on when the demon spoke out of the person and said, "Don't tell me about how they crucified Him; I was there when they did it!" Instantly, I said, "You are lying, demon!" Then I heard the Holy Spirit say, "Isaiah, the demon isn't lying; it was there." After some time the demon did finally leave, and the person was completely set free. I was shocked and realized these demons have been around for thousands of years; they have seen kings fall, empires collapse, and societies come and go. These are the same demons from ancient days!

Scripture is unclear about the origin of demons, but most people, including many scholars, lean toward them being fallen angels.[2] I don't want to spend more time speculating on the origin of demons, as it is not important; what's important is that we cast them out.

Let me clarify a few terms that we will use throughout this book. We will refer to demons as unclean spirits, fallen angels, and demonic spirits. When we use the word *deliverance*, we are using it to describe the casting out of demons. Some would call this an exorcism, and that is also correct; I just prefer to use the word *deliverance*. We will do our best to avoid the words *possessed* and *oppressed*. You will find out why, in a later chapter, we will instead use the word *demonized* to define someone who has a demon. Lastly, when we use the phrase "a demon manifested," we are simply describing a demon making itself known in a person. This could be through the demon talking, the person making animal noises or contorting in ways humanly impossible, or various other things.

As we conclude this chapter, remember that casting out demons is not just for a select few but is a calling for all believers. Mark 16:17 (KJV) clearly states, "And these signs shall follow them that believe; in my name shall they cast out devils." This means you have the authority and responsibility to free people, just as Jesus did.

If you are a follower of Christ, you are His ambassador, empowered to carry out His work on earth. Don't be content with merely knowing about this power—step into it, embrace it, and let God work through you to bring healing and deliverance to those around you. The same Spirit that raised Jesus from the dead lives in you, ready to break every chain and demolish every stronghold. It's time to rise up, cast out demons, and walk in the victory Christ has already secured for you.

Chapter 2

HOW JESUS CAST
OUT DEMONS

WHEN GOD GAVE me the vision to write this book, I knew the main thing I wanted to do at the beginning was look at every deliverance Jesus did in the New Testament and see what we can learn from it. I wanted the foundation of this entire book to be on Jesus' ministry.

Think about it: Who better to learn from than the One who instituted deliverance ministry? Jesus was the first person in Scripture to cast out demons. This was the only ministry He brought that was unique to Him. When Jesus arrived, the sick had already been healed in the Old Testament, miracles had taken place in the Old Testament, and the dead had even been raised in the Old Testament. But one specific ministry had never been done before, and that was the casting out of demons.

For the first time, the world experienced freedom from demonic bondage. In the Old Testament, God brought the people out of bondage, but in the New Testament, He brought the bondage out of the people. The very start of Jesus' ministry was Him immediately casting out demons. Mark 1:39 says, "So he traveled throughout the region of Galilee, preaching in the synagogues and casting out demons." I hesitate to call it deliverance ministry; a better name for it is the ministry of Jesus!

Did you know that deliverance is found in the atonement? Matthew 8:16–17 says something so interesting: "That evening many demon-possessed people were brought to Jesus. He cast out the evil spirits with a simple command, and he healed all the sick. This fulfilled the word of the Lord through the prophet Isaiah, who said, 'He took our sicknesses and removed our diseases.'"

Right there it shows that deliverance is part of the atonement. Jesus died not only so we could be saved but so we could be free *right now* from demonic bondage. Through the cross He has rescued us from spiritual death; through His suffering we get healing and deliverance of body and soul. Healing and deliverance are part of that provision. He paid such a high price for this, so why do we cheapen what He paid for? What if you understood that the same power that grants us eternal life is available to heal and deliver us? What if we didn't separate it but instead said come to the altar and get saved, delivered, and healed? First John 3:8 says, "But when people keep on sinning, it shows that they belong to the devil, who has been sinning since the beginning. *But the Son of God came to destroy the works of the devil*" (emphasis added). One of the main reasons Jesus came to earth was to set the captives free.

Accused of Being the Devil

One thing you can expect to happen when you start casting out demons is for people to accuse you of being the devil. This happens for a simple reason: They did it to Jesus, so they will do it to you! The first time Jesus is ever accused of being Satan is when He casts out demons. Matthew 12:24–28 (NKJV) says:

> Now when the Pharisees heard [that Jesus had delivered a man possessed by a blind and mute spirit,] they said, "This fellow does not cast out demons except by Beelzebub, the ruler of the demons." But Jesus knew their thoughts, and said to them: "Every kingdom divided against itself is brought to desolation, and every city or house divided against itself will not stand. If Satan casts out Satan, he is divided against himself. How then will his kingdom stand? And if I cast out demons by Beelzebub, by whom do your sons cast them out? Therefore they shall be your judges. But if I cast out demons by the Spirit of God, surely the kingdom of God has come upon you."

Jesus reveals to the Pharisees there is no way He could be doing this with demonic power because a kingdom that is divided cannot stand. I can't imagine how Jesus felt trying to help people yet being called a devil for doing so. Sadly, religious people do this all the time today. You will see as you start deliverance ministry that it is usually not those in the world who will oppose you but those inside the church. I love how Jesus ends this argument with the Pharisees. He says, "If I cast out demons by the Spirit of God, surely the kingdom of God has come upon you." Wow, what a powerful truth! Deliverance is the arrival of God's kingdom!

> When you start casting out demons you can expect people to accuse you of being the devil. They did it to Jesus, so they will do it to you!

Some translations say, "If I cast out demons by the finger of

God" instead of "the Spirit of God" (Luke 11:20). I like to tell people that when deliverance happens, it's the fingerprint of God on their life. Deliverance is not a bad or negative thing; it is not something we should be ashamed of. It is powerful and incredible when God sets someone free. The Christian life is not just "What would Jesus do?" but "Do what Jesus did!" John 14:12 says, "I tell you the truth, anyone who believes in me will do the same works I have done, and even greater works, because I am going to be with the Father."

Let's not even talk about the greater works. Let's just focus on the same works! Jesus clearly says we can do the works He has done, and yes, that includes casting out demons. I want you to notice it does not say the disciples, it does not say the apostles, it does not say "until I die on the cross"—there is no end to this. The prerequisite is "anyone who believes in me will do the same works." Do not believe the religious lie that this ended with the apostles.

SEVEN INSTANCES OF DELIVERANCE

Now let's look at the seven detailed instances of Jesus casting out demons and see what we can learn from them. In a later chapter I will outline my seven-step method for casting out demons, but as I said before, let's build the foundation on Jesus and learn as much as we can from how He did things. His way is the best way. This will no doubt be the most crucial portion of this entire book. We know that according to John 21:25, "Jesus also did many other things. If they were all written down, I suppose the whole world could not contain the books that would be written." So what we see in the Gospels is not *all* Jesus did. John said He did countless other things that we just don't have documented.

1. The demoniac in the synagogue (Mark 1:23 and Luke 4:31)

This is the very start of Jesus' ministry, in the seaside town of Capernaum, and He begins it by driving out a demon from a man inside the synagogue. Remember, these are not bystanders coming into the synagogue. These are devout Jews. Look what happens next:

> When the Sabbath day came, he went into the synagogue and began to teach. The people were amazed at his teaching, for he taught with real authority—quite unlike the teachers of religious law. Suddenly, a man in the synagogue who was possessed by an evil spirit cried out, "Why are you interfering with us, Jesus of Nazareth? Have you come to destroy us? I know who you are—the Holy One of God!" But Jesus reprimanded him. "Be quiet! Come out of the man," he ordered. At that, the evil spirit screamed, threw the man into a convulsion, and then came out of him. Amazement gripped the audience, and they began to discuss what had happened. "What sort of new teaching is this?" they asked excitedly. "It has such authority! Even evil spirits obey his orders!" The news about Jesus spread quickly throughout the entire region of Galilee.
>
> —MARK 1:21–28

Lesson 1: Jesus' powerful preaching caused this man to manifest the demon that had been living in him. This man had not manifested before because when preaching is weak and dull, demons are not threatened by it. Here comes Jesus preaching with power and authority, and all of a sudden demons surface. The Bible says He taught as one with authority, not as the teachers of the law. They were dull, they were laid-back, they did not preach with power and authority, and here comes Jesus with authority when He preaches. It's no wonder demons don't manifest in most church services today; they are dry! The crowd said,

"What is this? A new teaching? And He teaches with authority." Oftentimes when deliverance breaks out in a church or group of believers, religious people think it is some new teaching. One of the reasons I am writing this book and adding so much scripture is to show that deliverance is not a new teaching, only a forgotten teaching. When the Word of God is preached with power, demons can't help but reveal themselves and fear God.

Lesson 2: The demon screamed out of the man. The Scripture is referring to the demon screaming out, not the man; this is what you will see in deliverance—demons often scream out of people. They will take over people's bodies as this demon did. He took over the man's mouth and spoke out of him. We need to learn how to discern what is demonic and what is the Spirit of God. The person manifesting can't always tell. Just because someone is crying doesn't mean it's God moving; sometimes it's a demon crying out of them.

> When the Word of God is preached with power, demons can't help but reveal themselves and fear God.

By what he said, we can tell there is not only one demon but multiple. Sometimes by listening to how the demon talks, you can tell if there is more than one. Verse 24 says, "Why are you interfering with us, Jesus of Nazareth? Have you come to destroy us? I know who you are—the Holy One of God!" With *us* being plural, this was probably the chief demon speaking out of the man, and there were other demons under his command.

Lesson 3: Demons want nothing to do with Jesus. They hate Jesus, and they hate you because you resemble Him. They want to stay away from anyone or anyplace where His presence is manifesting. If you suddenly have friends or family that don't want to be around you, it's probably the demons in them wanting to avoid you. They know who you are when you start doing deliverance ministry.

Lesson 4: Jesus told the demon to be quiet. Jesus did this not because He was against us talking to demons—we know that later in Scripture He spoke to a demon—but because He didn't want the demon revealing to people who He was before it was revealed to them through revelation. This is why He would tell people He healed to be quiet and not tell anyone. From this account we also learn we have the power to tell a demon to be silent. If you can't get a demon to stop talking and manifesting, you can call the person by name and simply say, "I want to speak to Amanda," for example. Calling the person by their name will usually cause the demon to stop manifesting through them.

Lesson 5: Jesus did this in front of everyone during the service. He didn't take the man to the back room, although that is sometimes a good option. He dealt with the demon on the spot, and the Bible says the man shook violently and let out a loud screech. It is very common for someone to convulse during deliverance and scream when the demon leaves. Some people who say it should always be calm and quiet have not read the Gospels. Deliverance was often accompanied by dramatic manifestations.

What Jesus did here completely demolishes the idea that deliverance should not be done in front of people, that deliverance should not be loud or have manifestations, and that deliverance is not for inside the church; it's for outside. Look at the reaction of the people. The Bible says they were in awe. They were amazed, and news spread about Jesus. Deliverance causes people to be in awe of Jesus, in awe of His power. It is one of the most incredible things to witness because you are witnessing Satan's kingdom being destroyed and Jesus' kingdom being established.

2. The man at the tombs (Luke 8:26–35, Mark 5, and Matthew 8:28)

> Then they sailed to the country of the Gadarenes, which is opposite Galilee. And when He stepped out on the land, there met Him a certain man from the city who had demons for a long time. And he wore no clothes, nor did he live in a house but in the tombs. When he saw Jesus, he cried out, fell down before Him, and with a loud voice said, "What have I to do with You, Jesus, Son of the Most High God? I beg You, do not torment me!" For He had commanded the unclean spirit to come out of the man. For it had often seized him, and he was kept under guard, bound with chains and shackles; and he broke the bonds and was driven by the demon into the wilderness. Jesus asked him, saying, "What is your name?" And he said, "Legion," because many demons had entered him. And they begged Him that He would not command them to go out into the abyss. Now a herd of many swine was feeding there on the mountain. So they begged Him that He would permit them to enter them. And He permitted them. Then the demons went out of the man and entered the swine, and the herd ran violently down the steep place into the lake and drowned. When those who fed them saw what had happened, they fled and told it in the city and in the country. Then they went out to see what had happened, and came to Jesus, and found the man from whom the demons had departed, sitting at the feet of Jesus, clothed and in his right mind. And they were afraid.
> —LUKE 8:26–35, NKJV

It is clear from the text that this man was highly demonized and in today's society would be considered mentally ill. The Bible says he was living in the tombs, but if he was around today, it's likely he would live in a mental hospital. I have a cousin who worked for years in a mental hospital, and she told me heartbreaking stories of how demonized so many of the people were.

Many of those who are put aside and forgotten about in mental hospitals could be set free by the power of Christ. Deliverance is much needed in many of these facilities. Let us consider what we can learn from this passage when it comes to deliverance.

Lesson 1: He had supernatural strength. He could not be restrained by chains, the Bible says. This is something ubiquitous in deliverance. It will sometimes take three or four people to hold someone down because of the supernatural strength demons exhibit. I have seen people who weigh one hundred pounds give three or four people trouble in deliverance. We see this too in Acts 19 with the sons of Sceva, who when they tried to do deliverance were overpowered by an evil spirit "so that they fled out of that house naked and wounded" (v. 16, NKJV).

Use caution with this. Don't be scared, but don't be ignorant either. If you know you're going to do deliverance on someone larger, make sure to get help. This is one major area where angels come into play. Hebrews 1:14 is a verse you need to memorize: "Therefore, angels are only servants—spirits sent to care for people who will inherit salvation." So don't be afraid to ask the Father to send angels to help you. The biblical way to pray for angels is to ask the Father to send them. We don't pray to angels or worship them, but they are invaluable tools in warfare. In Matthew 26:53 Jesus said, "Don't you realize that I could ask my Father for thousands of angels to protect us, and he would send them instantly?" Think about that.

Lesson 2: The demon did not leave immediately. Notice what Luke 8:29 (ESV) says: "For he had commanded the unclean spirit to come out of the man." In the very next verse Jesus says, "What is your name?" There is a common error: People believe that demons will instantly leave the moment you tell them to. This is often repeated by people who have never done deliverance before. When you begin to actually do deliverance, you will learn that sometimes demons are stubborn and do not leave immediately. Later in this book I will dedicate an entire chapter to dealing with stubborn demons. Do not be discouraged if a demon does not leave the second you tell it to; this demon was even resisting and stubborn when Jesus told it to leave.

Lesson 3: He was like a wild animal. The Bible says nobody could tame the Gadarene demoniac. We have seen this in society as well. We see people walking down the street growling, which is a significant symptom of being demonized. I've lost track of how many people I've prayed for and they instantly started growling. I've had people say, "Every time you pray for me, I growl!" That is a demonic manifestation. I have seen many people act like animals in deliverance. I have seen birds, bulls, dogs, snakes, and other animals' spirits, primarily if the spirit of an animal will act like that animal.

One of the most common manifestations you will see when praying for deliverance is the person slithering like a snake. I probably don't need to remind you, but the snake in the Bible represents Satan. Luke 10:19 says, "Look, I have given you authority over all the power of the enemy, and you can walk among snakes and scorpions and crush them. Nothing will injure you." When the Bible says you can crush snakes and scorpions, it's not talking about real ones. It's talking about demonic spirits. Jesus has given us authority over these things.

Lesson 4: Jesus required the demon to identify itself by name. Jesus was not ignorant of who he was, and I don't think the information was even necessary for the deliverance. I think He did this to teach us an essential step in deliverance. When spirits are forced to name themselves, their power is weakened. Remember, the devil loses control when he is exposed, and by revealing his name and nature, Legion lost the power he had over the man. I tell people all the time the best thing that can happen is for you to know a demon is there hiding because now you can evict it. You can't evict someone if you don't even know they are living there.

In a weird way, unclean spirits are like dogs. You can yell at a dog all you want, but if you don't know its name, you have no authority over it. The moment you yell the dog's name, you get obedience. Sometimes knowing or having the demon's name is a valuable tool. Usually when a demon tells you its name, it is actually telling you its function. So if you ask a spirit, "What is your name?" and it says, "Anger," that is actually the function of the demon. Their names are not unique to them like my name or your name might be. The name is merely its function.

3. The man who was blind and mute (Matthew 12:22 and Luke 11:14)

> One day Jesus cast out a demon from a man who couldn't speak, and when the demon was gone, the man began to speak. The crowds were amazed, but some of them said, "No wonder he can cast out demons. He gets his power from Satan, the prince of demons." Others, trying to test Jesus, demanded that he show them a miraculous sign from heaven to prove his authority. He knew their thoughts, so he said, "Any kingdom divided by civil war is doomed. A family splintered by feuding will fall apart. You say I am empowered by Satan. But if Satan is divided and fighting against himself, how can his kingdom survive?"
>
> —LUKE 11:14–18

Lesson 1: These demons were preventing the man from speaking and seeing. Luke's Gospel says he couldn't speak, but Matthew's Gospel says he was blind and mute. This is what the devil wants to do to you: He does not want you to have a vision; he does not want you to see the plan and purpose God has for you. I've seen people with such powerful vision, and they've let demons steal their vision; they've let depression steal their vision; they've let anxiety steal their vision and steal their boldness to speak forth the gospel. Demons want to stop you from speaking, sharing, and declaring God's Word. They want to shut down your voice. This man physically couldn't see or speak, but demons do this to people all the time spiritually.

Lesson 2: People accused Jesus of being of Satan when He cast out demons. Luke 10:16 says, "Then he said to the disciples, 'Anyone who accepts your message is also accepting me. And anyone who rejects you is rejecting me. And anyone who rejects me is rejecting God, who sent me.'"

This was the last thing Jesus told the seventy-two disciples before He sent them out to preach and cast out demons. He knew the rejection they would face while preaching and doing deliverance because He experienced the exact same thing. It hurts to have friends, family, and the church reject you for doing what Jesus has told you to do, but this is all part of the suffering we partake in with Christ. Trust me when I say your family and friends will think you're crazy when you start participating in deliverance ministry, but you have to choose to be obedient to Christ over being obedient to them.

Lesson 3: A kingdom divided can't stand. Satan has a kingdom, and it works together in unity. When you do deliverance, you will realize how the demons tag-team and work together. One will go down, another comes up, and they work back and forth. Your deliverance team needs to be united. You cannot let the demons be more unified than you. You need to make sure only one person is leading the deliverance so there is no division or confusion; make sure nobody is arguing or in disunity in your group because the devil plays on disunity. We must work together. We must come together in unity to go against Satan. Unity is a powerful spiritual weapon.

Lesson 4: There was actual life change after the man was delivered: He was able to see, speak, and worship God. This was a dramatic change in his life. The beauty of deliverance is seeing the life change in people afterward and seeing the difference in how they live.

4. The man with the demonized son (Mark 9:14, Matthew 17:14, and Luke 9:37)

Then one of the crowd answered and said, "Teacher, I brought You my son, who has a mute spirit. And wherever it seizes him, it throws him down; he foams at the mouth, gnashes his teeth, and becomes rigid. So I spoke to Your disciples, that they should cast it out, but they could not." He answered him and said, "O faithless generation, how long shall I be with you? How long shall I bear with you? Bring him to Me." Then they brought him to Him. And when he saw Him, immediately the spirit convulsed him, and he fell on the ground and wallowed, foaming at the mouth. So He asked his father, "How long has this been happening to him?" And he said, "From childhood. And often he has thrown him both into the fire and into the water to destroy him. But if You can do anything, have compassion on us and help us." Jesus said to him, "If you can believe, all things are possible to him who believes." Immediately the father of the child cried out and said with tears, "Lord, I believe; help my unbelief!" When Jesus saw that the people came running together, He rebuked the unclean spirit, saying to it, "Deaf and dumb spirit, I command you, come out of him and enter him no more!" Then the spirit cried out, convulsed him greatly, and came out of him. And he became as one dead, so that many said, "He is dead." But Jesus took him by the hand and lifted him up, and he arose. And when He had come into the house, His disciples asked Him privately, "Why could

we not cast it out?" So He said to them, "This kind can come
out by nothing but prayer and fasting."

—MARK 9:17–29, NKJV

Lesson 1: The demon was trying to kill the boy. This is the
goal of a demon in a person's life. It cast the boy into both water
and fire, trying to destroy him. Demons want to destroy your
life. For some people complete deliverance is a matter of life and
death. There are countless documentaries of serial killers who
said, "A demon made me do it." It's not the demon that pulls the
trigger. It's the demon that gives them the overwhelming desire
until they finally give in. The ministry of deliverance is so serious
because people's lives are at stake.

Lesson 2: The demon manifested in foaming at the mouth,
convulsing, and falling on the ground. When Jesus cast it out, it
came out screaming, and the boy became as one who was dead, the Bible says. To the people who say, "Well, I won't let demons manifest when I cast them out," or, "These manifestations aren't biblical; tell it to leave," I think you must do it better than Jesus because even Jesus let the demon manifest. You don't get to choose if or how someone manifests. Sometimes it's dramatic, and sometimes it isn't. We don't care about manifestations. We care about freedom. It is not abnormal when a demon fully leaves a person for them to fall down as if dead, just as this boy did.

> For some people complete deliverance is a matter of life and death.

Lesson 3: Jesus commanded the demon out by name. He says
in verse 25, "Deaf and dumb spirit, I command you, come out
of him and enter him no more." Many people teach you not to

command them by name, or that the name doesn't matter. Well, Jesus commanded this demon out by name. They oftentimes respond to their name. You find out their name by either the Holy Spirit telling you or them saying their name, as we see with the man at the tombs. I will go into greater detail on this when I give my seven-step process for casting out demons.

Lesson 4: Jesus said this type only comes out by prayer and fasting. Being in deliverance ministry takes spiritual discipline. If you are lazy and don't have discipline, do not try to cast out demons. Some demons, or, as Jesus says, some types of demons, are stronger and able to withstand those who do not have a life of prayer and fasting. I believe prayer and fasting are essential to incorporate into your life if you want to be effective at casting out demons.

5. The Syrophoenician woman's daughter (Mark 7:24 and Matthew 15:21)

> From there He arose and went to the region of Tyre and Sidon. And He entered a house and wanted no one to know it, but He could not be hidden. For a woman whose young daughter had an unclean spirit heard about Him, and she came and fell at His feet. The woman was a Greek, a Syro-Phoenician by birth, and she kept asking Him to cast the demon out of her daughter. But Jesus said to her, "Let the children be filled first, for it is not good to take the children's bread and throw it to the little dogs." And she answered and said to Him, "Yes, Lord, yet even the little dogs under the table eat from the children's crumbs." Then He said to her, "For this saying go your way; the demon has gone out of your daughter." And when she had come to her house, she found the demon gone out, and her daughter lying on the bed.
>
> —MARK 7:24–30, NKJV

It's important to note this woman was not eligible for deliverance because she was a Greek and not a Jew. Jesus first ministered to the Jews. This is why He said to let the "children" be filled first. She responded that even the dogs (Greeks) sit under the table and eat the children's (Jews') crumbs. Jesus was so shocked by her faith that He said even though originally she was not eligible for her daughter to be delivered, her faith in Him has made her eligible. Her daughter has been set free.

Lesson 1: Children can be demonized. The Greek word for *daughter* in this passage signifies a very young child. This is so common, yet not discussed or preached in the church. So many kids need deliverance, and we don't even think twice about it. In fact, two out of the seven deliverances documented in the Gospels were of children. The devil wants to kill our kids while they are young. Why do you think so many kids' shows are filled with witchcraft and gender confusion? The devil has a target on our kids. Stop pulling the wool over your eyes, and get aggressive. If you don't fight for your kids, who will? We sit around while the enemy sneaks in and infiltrates our children. If you don't get involved in deliverance for others, do it for them! Our children deserve to be set free.

Lesson 2: Parents are not only physical guardians of their kids but spiritual guardians. Parents are able to petition Jesus for their children's deliverance. What's interesting is that Jesus did this deliverance at a distance at the mother's request. This should give every parent hope for their kids. I believe there is a special grace for deliverance to happen to kids even if they're not at the meeting or with a deliverance minister present.

Lesson 3: Faith is essential to deliverance. In Matthew 15:28 (NKJV), Jesus says, "O woman, great is your faith! Let it be to you as you desire." Faith is required for salvation, healing, baptism of the Spirit, and deliverance. The worst thing you can do at the start of a deliverance is say, "I don't think I'm going to get free today." You might as well go home. The devil always lies in deliverance, saying you won't be free. That is him attacking your faith because he knows how powerful a weapon faith is. The Syrophoenician woman was not an unbeliever. She called Jesus Lord and asked for a blessing from her master's table. Her entire demeanor says she was a believer. A person can receive deliverance based on someone else but must retain deliverance in their own faith.

6. The mute man (Matthew 9:32–34)

> While they were going out, a man who was demon-possessed and could not talk was brought to Jesus. And when the demon was driven out, the man who had been mute spoke. The crowd was amazed and said, "Nothing like this has ever been seen in Israel." But the Pharisees said, "It is by the prince of demons that he drives out demons."
> —MATTHEW 9:32–34, NIV

There is only one thing I want to point out in this deliverance: People were shocked because they had never seen anything like this. You will find this, especially in the church—the place where deliverance should be happening. People will be shocked because they haven't seen it. To the doubting pastor or believer who is reading this, just because you haven't seen or experienced it does not mean it isn't real! We need to be open to allowing Jesus to do whatever He wants to do, even if that means doing something we have never seen before.

7. The woman with the spirit of infirmity (Luke 13:10–17)

> Now He was teaching in one of the synagogues on the Sabbath. And behold, there was a woman who had a spirit of infirmity eighteen years, and was bent over and could in no way raise

herself up. But when Jesus saw her, He called her to Him and said to her, "Woman, you are loosed from your infirmity." And He laid His hands on her, and immediately she was made straight, and glorified God. But the ruler of the synagogue answered with indignation, because Jesus had healed on the Sabbath; and he said to the crowd, "There are six days on which men ought to work; therefore come and be healed on them, and not on the Sabbath day." The Lord then answered him and said, "Hypocrite! Does not each one of you on the Sabbath loose his ox or donkey from the stall, and lead it away to water it? So ought not this woman, being a daughter of Abraham, whom Satan has bound—think of it—for eighteen years, be loosed from this bond on the Sabbath?" And when He said these things, all His adversaries were put to shame; and all the multitude rejoiced for all the glorious things that were done by Him.

—Luke 13:10–17, nkjv

Lesson 1: Christians often need deliverance. Now, this woman was not a New Testament believer in the sense that she had received the Holy Spirit, because the Holy Spirit had not been poured out yet, but she definitely was a believer in God. This deliverance happened inside a synagogue, which would be like a modern-day church. They would meet on the Sabbath to worship and be taught the Word of God. The woman with the spirit of infirmity was a worshipper, not some random bystander.

The need for deliverance is often found among genuine believers, not on the street corner. The idea that deliverance is only for people heavily involved in the occult or criminal activity is not the case. Many genuine God-loving and God-fearing believers need deliverance. Nowhere in Scripture does it say if you are a believer in Jesus, the devil cannot demonize you. I will dedicate an entire chapter to showing how Christians *can* be demonized.

Lesson 2: Demons cause infirmities. Many sicknesses can be attributed to demonic spirits. Not all sicknesses, of course, but often in the Gospels people would bring the sick to Jesus, and He would cast demons out of them. This woman, for eighteen years, was bent over and could not stand straight. Just imagine all the medications and treatments she had tried. But nothing natural can cure a supernatural condition. Jesus cast out spirits of blindness, muteness, deafness, epilepsy, and fever. Remember, Jesus healed many people, and there was no mention of deliverance, so understand that Jesus is both our healer and our deliverer. We pray, and the Holy Spirit often reveals the remedy or the person's needs.

Lesson 3: Manifestations of demons are not always evident. One of the most common questions we get is "Does there have to be a manifestation?" and the answer is no. There is no mention of a manifestation here. Manifestations often occur in deliverance, but they are not necessary for the person to be set free. Our end goal is not getting people to manifest. It's getting people free. If they don't manifest, praise God. If they do, praise God; we want people free either way—however that looks. No two deliverances are the same. We cannot go into a deliverance with a preconceived notion of how it will go because I have learned through experience that it usually does not go how you think it will. What is important is to go in with a clear mind and let the Holy Spirit do whatever He wants to do.

Lesson 4: Jesus laid His hands on her. I have heard people preach against the laying on of hands in deliverance, even saying this is not scriptural. But clearly the Bible says in Luke 13 that He laid His hands upon her. Jesus often laid hands on those He ministered to. It is not required, but I have found it helpful and laid on hands whenever possible. As I've said before, you must be led by the Spirit and not restricted by methods. We should not be afraid of getting someone's demons by laying on hands.

Remember, demons can come only through open doors. As long as you don't have open doors, the demon cannot enter you.

I want to reiterate that not every miracle Jesus did is recorded. These are just the seven we have to study and learn from. There are many lessons to be learned from many great deliverance ministers, but Jesus is the greatest; He is the best teacher and leader to follow. I would challenge you to dive into these stories on your own and ask the Holy Spirit to reveal insight regarding deliverance ministry.

The ministry of deliverance was one of the main things Jesus focused on. It was not a minor ministry but a major one. Let us follow in His steps and make this ministry important in our lives as well.

Chapter 3

CHRISTIANS CAN HAVE DEMONS! EXPOSING THE LIE

T HERE IS NO doubt that the biggest point of contention over the ministry of deliverance is whether a Christian can have a demon. Most people in the modern church believe Christians *cannot* have demons, thereby cutting them off from the opportunity to receive deliverance in the first place. If you don't believe it's even possible for you or others as Christians to have demons, then you will never even seek deliverance or attempt to pray for those in need of freedom.

I believe the greatest lie the devil has spread throughout the church is that Christians can't have a demon. This has effectively allowed him to demonize our churches with no resistance, no fight, and no confrontation. This argument can get very heated and emotional, so I'm asking you to hear me out and look at the case I present before putting this book down because you don't agree with my stance.

In Don Dickerman's book *When Pigs Move In*, a book that

heavily inspired me to write this one, he says, "The presence of the Holy Spirit does not prevent evil spirits from dwelling in a believer's body or soul! Until a believer can recognize and understand how demonic bondage occurs, he cannot be free. You can be Spirit-filled, memorize the Word of God, sing in the choir, teach Sunday school, and be a deacon, teacher, or preacher, but you still have demons. I deal with this almost daily! That believers cannot have demons is a dangerous, widely held but false belief. It is a myth."[1]

Those who believe this lie are effectively saying deliverance is only for unbelievers and if you're a believer, you're not able to be set free. Think about how crazy that sounds. If I want freedom, I must be an unbeliever because if I'm a Christian, deliverance isn't for me. After all, if Christians couldn't have demons, there would be no need for deliverance in the first place. If this were the case, our goal would be to get people saved, and all their demons would leave, so why would there be a need to do deliverance after that point? It makes no sense, and I'm going to do my best to explain why I know—not believe but know—Christians can have demons. I say I *know* because there is a difference between knowing and believing. You have to believe something first, and then once you know it, you no longer have to believe.

> I believe the greatest lie the devil has spread throughout the church is that Christians can't have a demon.

KNOWING VERSUS BELIEVING

Let me give you an example. Say there is an old car in a garage somewhere, and you ask me, "Do you believe this car will start?" Because I've never seen the car start before, I might say I believe it'll start. The owner then starts the car, and now I go from believing it will start to knowing it will start. If you ask me the question again—"Do you believe this car will start?"—I will respond, "I know it will start because I have seen the car start before." In the same way, I know Christians can have demons because I've seen thousands of genuine Spirit-filled Christians be delivered from demons. I know not only because of my experience but also because I believe the Word of God teaches that deliverance is for the believer. So why is there so much confusion around this topic? A few reasons; the first one is because of *semantics.*

Many people don't believe Christians can have demons because of confusion around the word *possessed.* Much misunderstanding results from the King James Version having translated the Greek word *daimonizomai* as "possessed with devils." The actual Greek translation of *daimonizomai* is "to be under the power of a demon." There is a massive difference between being possessed—that is, being owned by a demon—and being demonized, or under the power of a demon. To be clear, Christians cannot be possessed by a demon in the sense of being owned by a demon, but I also don't believe the devil or a demon can own anything.

The right question we should be asking is not "Can a Christian be demon possessed?" but "Can a Christian have a demon or be under the power of demons?" To that I would say absolutely. If you open a door and give the devil a legal right, he will come in. The New Testament never makes a distinction when speaking of demonization between being oppressed or possessed, and we should not either. To avoid confusion, I recommend taking the words *oppressed* and *possessed* out of your vocabulary when discussing deliverance.

Most people believe Christians can be oppressed, and the image they have in their mind is of a demon being on someone's back or somehow influencing them from the outside. The problem is we never see this in Scripture; never once do we see Jesus casting demons off people, only out of people. That means principally demons live only inside of people and never live on the outside, in some way oppressing them. Oppression does exist in Scripture but not in relation to deliverance or the context of casting out demons. Sam Storms, a minister and author with more than thirty years of ministry experience, has a very informative article titled "Can a Christian Be Demonized?" that I can't recommend enough. In it he says:

> What's important for us to note is that every case of demonization involves someone under the influence or control, in varying degrees, of an *indwelling* evil spirit. The word "demonization" is never used in the NT to describe someone who is merely oppressed or harassed, attacked, or tempted by a demon. In every case, reference is made to a demon either entering, dwelling in, or being cast out of the person. Matthew 4:24 and 15:22 at first appear to be exceptions to this rule, but the parallel passages in Mark 1:32 and 7:24–30 indicate otherwise. Hence, to be "demonized," in the strict sense of that term, is to be inhabited by a demon with varying degrees of influence or control. On sixteen occasions in the NT, a reference is made to a person who "has" a demon. It is twice used by John the Baptist by his accusers (Matt. 11:18; Luke 7:33). Six times the enemies of Jesus use it of him (Mark 3:30; Jn. 7:20; 8:48, 49, 52; 10:20). Eight times it describes someone under the influence of a demonic spirit (Mark 5:15; 7:25; 9:17; Luke 4:33; 8:27; Acts 8:7; 16:16; 19:13). Hence to "have" a demon is to be "demonized" or inhabited by a demon (see

especially John 10:20–21). In summary, if a demon indwells or inhabits a person it is a case of demonization. Merely to be tempted, harassed, afflicted, or oppressed by a demon is not demonization. *Demonization always entails indwelling.*[2]

The point Storms makes in this article, and the point I'm trying to make, is that if a person has a demon, then it is living inside of them, not merely on them. When someone comes to tell me they have a demon and need deliverance, my job is not to question their salvation or convince them Christians can't have demons; my job is to help them get free. One woman told me she went to her pastor and said, "Pastor, will you pray for me? I think I have a demon; I have constant voices telling me to kill myself." This lady was a born-again Christian who had been a part of the church for a long time, but the problem was that her pastor, like so many people, didn't believe Christians could even have demons. So now he was obligated to put her salvation in question and say maybe you're not truly a Christian. How sad is that! Instead of casting the demon out of her and putting the demon on trial, her salvation was put on trial and in question because of a pastor with poor theology.

DELIVERANCE AT A LEADERSHIP RETREAT

I got invited once to speak to about forty pastors and leaders at a church retreat. This was a large church, and everyone there was a pastor or leader in some capacity at this church. I was a bit intimidated because the pastor had told me years prior about all the leadership speakers they had. These were big-name leadership speakers, and I thought, "How will I fill those shoes?" To make matters worse, I was supposed to speak to these leaders in back-to-back sessions, two hours in the morning and two hours in the afternoon. I thought, "Four hours of talking to the same small group of leaders? What could I possibly tell them that they don't already know?"

A few days before the retreat, I asked the lead pastor if he wanted me to talk about anything specifically, and he said, "How about deliverance?" I said great—not knowing almost all the pastors didn't believe Christians can have demons. I told the pastor, "I'm warning you, though, as I begin to teach on this, many of your pastors and leaders will likely manifest demons." He was confused by that statement, but he was soon to discover how true it was.

We started session one, and I went through my typical teachings about how every Christian is called to deliverance, why Christians need deliverance, how demons get in, and so forth. As I taught, I noticed many of them walking in and out and looking unsettled. The first session ended, and it was time for a short break. The lead pastor came up to me and said that while I was teaching, many of the pastors were leaving because they felt sick to their stomachs and needed to throw up. Others said they heard demonic voices telling them not to listen to this! He said, "Oh my gosh, Isaiah, they are manifesting just like you said. Can you teach the second session on deliverance?" I said no problem.

I ended up teaching for a total of six hours on deliverance and then stayed in the hotel lobby with most of those pastors until 1 a.m., answering every question you can think of about deliverance. All of them started that day not believing Christians can have demons but ended up realizing how much many of them needed deliverance. The pastor invited me the next weekend to take all of them through deliverance. I brought my good friend, who often does deliverance with me, and we stayed for three days and did extensive deliverance on all those leaders for twelve hours each day.

On the last day, the senior pastor brought me into his office with tears in his eyes and said, "I can't believe I've been in ministry for forty-plus years and never knew how much Christians need deliverance." Remember, these were not average churchgoers we were praying for. These were his leaders! You might be thinking, "But this is just your experience, and experience doesn't matter."

The argument that experience doesn't matter is very poor for a few reasons. First, the entire Gospels are about the experiences the disciples had with Jesus. Second, no matter what you believe, whether Christians can or can't have demons, you probably arrived at that belief based on your own life experiences. A person with an experience is never at the mercy of a person with an argument.

When John the Baptist was in prison and doubted Jesus was truly the One they were waiting for, surprisingly, this was after he baptized Jesus and declared, "Behold the lamb of God, who takes away the sins of the world." He sent his disciples to see if Jesus truly was the One or if they should be looking for someone else. Look at what Jesus tells them in Luke 7:20–22:

> John's two disciples found Jesus and said to him, "John the Baptist sent us to ask, 'Are you the Messiah we've been expecting, or should we keep looking for someone else?'" At that very time, Jesus cured many people of their diseases, illnesses, and evil spirits, and he restored sight to many who were blind. Then he told John's disciples, "Go back to John and tell him what you have seen and heard—the blind see, the lame walk, those with leprosy are cured, the deaf hear, the dead are raised to life, and the Good News is being preached to the poor."

Jesus did not tell them to go back and quote a scripture; He did not tell them to go back and share what He had said. He said to go back and tell them what they had experienced! What you have seen with your own eyes is that people with diseases were cured; the blind can see, the lame can walk, and the deaf can hear. It was the experiences that held weight. This is why I don't understand when people say, "Well, Isaiah's experiences don't matter when it comes to Christians having demons." Yes, they do! Jesus said in John 10:38, when the people would not believe He was who He said He was, "But if I do his work, believe in the evidence of the miraculous works I have done, even if you don't believe me. Then you will know and understand that the Father is in me, and I am in the Father." Jesus was saying *believe the miraculous experiences.*

But What About Spirit-Filled Christians?

Some might argue that we do not see any Spirit-filled New Testament Christians getting delivered in Scripture. Some would say this is an argument from silence, meaning just because the Bible doesn't state something clearly doesn't mean it's not real. I would agree with that, but I would also say it's clear there are believers who received deliverance in Scripture. For example, all seven of the deliverances I

> A person with an experience is never at the mercy of a person with an argument.

mentioned earlier concerning Jesus involved people who believed in Him in one capacity or another. Were they Spirit-filled New Testament believers? The answer is no because Jesus had not died and the Holy Spirit had not been poured out yet. But did they believe in Him? Yes. Let's look at the biblical model of evangelism for a moment.

There is only one man in all of Scripture who is an evangelist by title, and that is Philip. This doesn't mean there weren't other evangelists. It simply means the Bible only states clearly that Philip was an evangelist. Acts 21:8 says, "The next day we went on to Caesarea and stayed at the home of Philip the Evangelist, one of the seven men who had been chosen to distribute food." We know Philip is an evangelist, so let's see how he evangelizes. Acts 8:5–8 (NKJV) says,

> Then Philip went down to the city of Samaria and preached Christ to them. And the multitudes with one accord heeded the things spoken by Philip, hearing and seeing the miracles which he did. For unclean spirits, crying with a loud voice, came out of many who were possessed; and many who were paralyzed and lame were healed. And there was great joy in that city.

OK, so let's get this straight: First Philip preached, and then with one accord the people heeded the things he spoke, and then Philip prayed for the sick and cast out demons. If Christians couldn't have demons, why would Philip even waste his time casting out demons? Wouldn't he get everyone saved, and the demons would automatically leave? Here we see in the early church, in the New Covenant, a need for deliverance.

Let's look at another instance where I believe the Bible makes it clear Christians can be demonized (not possessed, mind you). In Acts 4:31 some of the early disciples had a prayer meeting, and then something remarkable happened. The text says, "After this prayer, the meeting place shook, and they were all filled with the Holy Spirit. Then they preached the word of God with boldness."

So now we know for sure they are Spirit-filled. Later in the chapter, they start selling all their property and giving the money to the apostles to distribute and meet needs. A couple named Ananias and Sapphira decide they are going to keep some of the money from the property they sold but claim they gave all the money. Acts 5:3 says, "Then Peter said, 'Ananias, why have you let Satan fill your heart? You lied to the Holy Spirit, and you kept some of the money for yourself.'" Here we see that in Acts 4 they were filled with the Holy Spirit, but one chapter later Peter says Ananias has let Satan fill his heart. This shows the possibility of a Spirit-filled believer being filled with something demonic. The word *filled* in Acts 4 is the same Greek word used in Acts 5. The example is clear: A Spirit-filled believer chose to lie to the Holy Spirit and in turn allowed himself to be filled with an unholy spirit.

Paul warns the church in Corinth that he's afraid they are going to receive a demonic spirit.

> But I fear that somehow your pure and undivided devotion to Christ will be corrupted, just as Eve was deceived by the cunning ways of the serpent. You happily put up with whatever anyone tells you, even if they preach a different Jesus than the one we preach, or a different kind of Spirit than the one you received, or a different kind of gospel than the one you believed.
>
> —2 CORINTHIANS 11:3–4

If Christians cannot have demons, why would Paul worry about them receiving a different kind of spirit? It's clear if you open yourself up to other spirits, they will come in whether you're a Christian or not. In 1 Timothy 4:1 (NKJV), Paul warns Timothy that in times coming, Christians will give in to demons. He says, "Now the Spirit expressly says that in latter times some will depart from the faith, giving heed to deceiving spirits and doctrines of demons." Once again, if Christians can't have demons, why would Paul feel the need to warn of giving heed to deceiving (demonic) spirits?

INSIDE THE SAME BODY?

Some might wonder how a demon and the Holy Spirit can live inside the same body. I believe the Holy Spirit dwells in your spirit when you're born again, and any demons dwell in the realm of your soul. This is your mind, will, and emotions. Paul tells the church in Thessalonica they are three parts: "And the God of peace himself sanctify you wholly; and may your spirit and soul and body be preserved entire, without blame at the coming of our Lord Jesus Christ" (1 Thess. 5:23, ASV). So we are spirit, soul, and body—tri-part beings—and the area demons dwell in is the part still being renewed, the soul. To say that the Holy Spirit can't dwell where a demon is also is a stretch, in my opinion. I want to refer to another excerpt in Sam Storms' article that I mentioned earlier:

> The second argument is that this would be a "spiritual" impossibility. That is to say, "How can the *Holy* Spirit inhabit the same body with an *unholy* demon?" But again, we must remember that the Holy Spirit, in a certain sense, "inhabits" everything. The Holy Spirit is, after all, omnipresent. He dwells everywhere! You may also recall from the book of Job that Satan had access to the presence of God, indicating that the issue is not one of spatial proximity but of *personal relationship.* The Holy Spirit and demons are in close proximity when outside the human body, so why could they not be in close proximity while inside one? Finally, the Holy Spirit indwells the Christian even though the latter still has a sinful nature or sinful flesh. In other words, if the *Holy* Spirit can inhabit the same body with *unholy* human sin, why could he not inhabit the same body with an *unholy* demon?
>
> It strikes me that the force of this argument appears to be more emotional than biblical. The idea of the Holy Spirit and a demon living inside a believer is *too close, too intimate* of contact. The thought of it is emotionally provocative and

scandalous; it violates one's sense of spiritual propriety. The *feeling* is that God simply wouldn't allow it. His love for his own is too great to let demonic influence get that far. But we must always keep in mind that the only criterion for making a decision on an issue such as this is not what *seems* or *feels* proper to us but what the Scripture explicitly asserts.[3]

Storms does a great job of explaining how the Holy Spirit and a demon can certainly dwell in the same place.

Another reason I believe Christians can have demons is in relation to the story of the Syrophoenician woman that we discussed in the previous chapter. John Eckhardt has a great take on this from an article in *Charisma* magazine titled "Can a Christian Have a Demon?" Concerning this story, he says:

> The story of the Syrophoenician woman in Mark 7:25–30 makes this clear. The woman sought out Jesus so He would deliver her daughter from an unclean spirit. But Jesus told her, "'Let the children be filled first, for it is not good to take the children's bread and throw it to the little dogs'" (v. 27).
>
> In this verse the phrase "the children's bread" refers specifically to deliverance, and Jesus is saying it belongs to His covenant people. Those outside the covenant may receive a miracle based on God's mercy, but deliverance is meant for those who have a covenant with God. Luke 1:71–73 says Jesus came "that we should be saved from our enemies and from the hand of all who hate us, to perform the mercy promised to our fathers and to remember His holy covenant, the oath which He swore to our father Abraham." He brought salvation from our enemies—devils and demons—based on a promise, of which we are heirs (see Gal. 3:29), that He made to Abraham.
>
> The purpose of this salvation is stated in subsequent verses of Luke 1: "To grant us that we, being delivered from the hand of our enemies, might serve Him without fear, in holiness and righteousness before Him, all the days of our life" (vv. 74–75).

> God provides the benefit so that we may serve Him without
> fear, in holiness and in righteousness all the days of our lives.
> It is very difficult to live this way without being delivered. In
> fact, it is practically impossible.[4]

At the end of the day, some people reading this could see
every verse, listen to every argument, and hear every teaching
we have on this topic but still not be convinced until they experience it. There is something experience does that nothing else
can do. A pastor friend told me he had another pastor over, and
as they were talking and just hanging out, my name came up.
My pastor's friend, who is also a friend of mine, said, "Oh, I
really like Isaiah Saldivar, except I don't believe Christians can
have demons, and because he teaches that they can, I really
don't listen to him or recommend him."

My pastor friend humbly disagreed and tried to tell him why
we believed that. An hour or two went by, and the guy shared
some struggles he'd been having, so my pastor friend said, "Do
you mind if I pray for you?" The guy said sure, and they began
to pray. My pastor friend began to call out any demonic spirits
that were hiding, and sure enough, the man started to manifest
a demon. My pastor friend took him through deliverance, and
afterward he said, "I can't believe all this time I thought Isaiah
was crazy for believing Christians can have demons, and I had a
demon myself!"

Guess what? He now believes Christians can have demons. I
can exhaust you with hundreds of stories of Christians having
demons, but at the end of the day you have to decide you're
willing to be wrong on this topic and say, "God, open my eyes
and reveal the truth to me." Sadly, this lie has kept countless
people in bondage. I'm praying that God will open the eyes of the
body of Christ and they will see the need for deliverance inside
the church.

Chapter 4

HOW DEMONS GET IN: SEVEN COMMON WAYS

O NE OF THE biggest struggles my wife and I have during the summertime is getting our kids to keep the doors closed. Having four young kids constantly going inside, then outside, then inside, then outside, I must yell, "Shut the door!" at least thirty times a day. They don't understand why I constantly tell them this, but I do. It's not because I'm trying to keep something in the house but because I'm trying to keep something out.

We left the house one summer day, and one of the kids left the back door open. We came home that night to countless flies, mosquitoes, and who knows what other types of bugs. In a house of five girls, who do you think was killing all those bugs? You guessed it: Dad. It took me several days to kill all the flies and mosquitoes that were let in because of that open door. This is precisely the way things work in the spiritual realm when it comes to demons. They are stalking and waiting for an open door so they can enter your house. When I say house, I do not mean your physical house; I mean your spiritual house, which is your body.

In Matthew 12:44 Jesus describes demons entering a human body as a demon entering a home. It says, "Then [the demon] says, 'I will return to the person I came from.' So it returns and finds its former home empty, swept, and in order." Later in this book I will give a complete breakdown of this passage, but what I want to emphasize is that demons consider our bodies their home. They crave a body to live in. I don't fully understand how this all works, but I will tell you that demons hate being without a body to live in. I believe it's because they need human faculties to accomplish their work. A spirit of addiction needs a human mouth to drink or smoke what it craves, a spirit of lust needs eyes to watch its perverted entertainment through, a spirit of murder needs hands to kill, and a spirit of anger needs the heart to fill with rage and destruction. Spirits need human bodies to work through. Their problem is they cannot enter into a human body without an open door.

In this chapter I want to establish common doors people open that give demons a legal right to be there. We must be hypervigilant and not open doors to demons, because when we open a door, we don't get to choose what comes through it. Proverbs 26:2 says, "Like a fluttering sparrow or a darting swallow, an undeserved curse will not land on its intended victim." This verse says there must be a cause for a curse to land; you cannot get a curse or a demon for no reason. There is always a door the demon must enter to access a person's life. Most people open doors unknowingly. That is why we must pinpoint how demons are getting in.

Evil Opportunists

The devil and his demons are opportunists. They are constantly looking for a weakness, an open door, or a moment of vulnerability to pounce. First Peter 5:8 (AMP) says, "Be sober [well balanced and self-disciplined], be alert and cautious at all times. That enemy of yours, the devil, prowls around like a roaring lion [fiercely hungry], seeking someone to devour."

Because the devil is the prince of demons and his demons mimic his behavior, when you see a verse describing the devil, you can be sure his demons function in the same way. Peter paints a picture of the devil as walking around looking for someone to devour. He is looking for an opportunity, an open door. The key is to be sober. "Why use the word *sober*?" you might wonder. Well, when you're under the influence of alcohol or drugs, you're no longer in control. Something else is now in control. Peter is saying that you need to remain self-controlled and not under the control of another force. You can no longer let anger, bitterness, lust, resentment, or anything else drive your life. Let these demons know right now, "You're no longer in control of me! I am sobering up."

The Bible does not say the devil is a roaring lion; it says he is "like" a roaring lion. There is only one true lion in Scripture: the lion of the Judah tribe! Revelation 5:5 says, "But one of the twenty-four elders said to me, 'Stop weeping! Look, the Lion of the tribe of Judah, the heir to David's throne, has won the victory. He is worthy to open the scroll and its seven seals.'" This is describing Christ as our Lord and Savior. Satan will try to

> Most people open doors unknowingly. That is why we must pinpoint how demons are getting in.

be "like" Christ but is nowhere near as powerful. Christ is seeking to save, and Satan is doing the exact opposite. He is looking for someone to devour. The interesting thing about Peter warning us of this is that he was one of the devil's main targets. You better believe Peter knows a thing or two about Satan and his evil schemes.

Satan approached Jesus, asking to destroy Simon Peter. Look at what Jesus said in Luke 22:31–32: "Simon, Simon, Satan has asked to sift each of you like wheat. But I have pleaded in prayer for you, Simon, that your faith should not fail. So when you have repented and turned to me again, strengthen your brothers." Back then you sifted wheat by putting it on a threshing floor, usually made of concrete, and beating it with a flail. This was to separate the trash (chaff) from the edible grain. Jesus was saying, "Peter, Satan is going to try and wear you out, beat you down, and ultimately get you to quit. The only thing that will get you through his pressing and crushing is having strong faith." Jesus reminds Peter that He is praying for him.

What a powerful thing to remember that even in our hardest moments Jesus is praying for us. Hebrews 7:25 says, "He is able, once and forever, to save those who come to God through him. He lives forever to intercede with God on their behalf." But even with this powerful promise, we must remember to be sober and have self-control if we want to make sure the doors stay closed to the enemy. History tells us that Peter lacked self-control and eventually fell into temptation and denied Jesus. Peter's warning is given not out of ignorance but out of personal experience.

Proverbs 25:28 (ESV) gives us insight into why we must have self-control in resisting the enemy. It says, "A man without self-control is like a city broken into and left without walls." So a man with no self-control is no different from a city with nothing to keep enemies out. The city is left without defenses; its doors are open, its gates are down, it can now be pillaged, and it can't even defend itself from the attackers.

In biblical times walls around a city were vital in keeping enemy nations out of that city. When those walls were gone, any surrounding enemy could freely gain entrance. This verse relates a man to a city; a man without self-control is vulnerable to demonic intrusion. In the same way this man is open to enemy attack, we too will be open to attack by the devil and his demons if we don't develop self-control in keeping doors closed.

Another scripture I want you to see relates to gates/doors.

GATES AND DOORS

Genesis 4:7 says, "You will be accepted if you do what is right. But if you refuse to do what is right, then watch out! Sin is crouching at the door, eager to control you. But you must subdue it and be its master." This was written long before 1 Peter 5:8 and even before Proverbs 25:28, yet we see the principle of doors back in Genesis. Do you see this connection? How badly sin wants to enter your house and control you, but you must be its master and subdue it. If this verse yelled a phrase, I think it would be, "Don't open the door!"

We've all probably seen horrifying videos of someone dressed as a delivery driver, and the moment the resident opens the door, they break in and rob that house. This is the terrifying reality of how demons and sin function. They wait at the door for you to open it so they can flood in with destruction. Ephesians 4:27 (NASB) says, "Do not give the devil an opportunity." Do not give the devil an opportunity to enter into your life, because if you do, he will gladly take it.

I'm going to show you some of the main ways demons gain entrance into people's lives, but before I do, I want you to remove the word *fair* from your vocabulary. When I show you some of the most common ways I have seen people demonized, you will immediately think, "Well, that doesn't seem fair," and you're right—it's not fair. The problem is the devil and his demons do not play fair. The word *fair* does not exist to him. He is evil and bent on destruction; he doesn't stop to check if what he's doing is ethical or fair. His goal is to bring maximum destruction to someone's life. He does not play by the rules. He takes pride in breaking the rules.

When I first got into deliverance ministry and saw the way the devil ruined lives and entered families, I couldn't understand how this could be, but then God revealed to me that the devil has been breaking the rules since the beginning. That is why he was cast out of heaven. He wanted to do his own thing, play by his rules, and now he tries to convince humanity to do the same. Think back to Genesis. He got Adam and Eve to break the rules! He got cast out of heaven for breaking the rules and then got Adam and Eve cast out of Eden for breaking the rules! His demons are rule breakers.

I will admit, the process of a demon entering into a human being is still a bit of a mystery to me, as nobody knows it all. If someone claims to have all the answers regarding the spiritual realm, they lie. I have found that when a demon enters a human, sometimes people feel it tangibly. Other times they have no idea what just happened.

I can remember an experience I had before I came to Christ where I had just done something extremely sinful and felt a weird presence enter me. I now believe it was a demon entering me, but at the time I was clueless. I can recall looking into the mirror other times and feeling as if someone was looking through my eyes. Once again, I was clueless at the time, but now I know it was a demon looking through my eyes. My point is we don't always know the moment a demon makes an entrance or even uses our bodies. Often when something happens in the spiritual realm, there is no indication in the natural realm.

Before we go into common open doors to demons, let me explain one last thing. Not every time you do one of these acts does a demon enter, but you do give a demon the opportunity to enter. You might practice one of these sinful things once and get a demon, or you might practice it fifty times and get nothing. I'm not sure why this is, but I must tell you that.

I am baffled by how some people have no demons even though they spent years doing sinful acts. I can recall praying for one girl who spent years practicing the occult and New Age yet had no demons when we took her through an extensive deliverance. I thought surely there must be something there, but for some reason there wasn't. "Why is that?" you might ask. Maybe she was delivered sovereignly by God, which does happen, or maybe a demon just never chose to enter her. I will never know the answer, but I do know that sometimes demons do not enter even if a door is opened. Let's now look at the first common door demons enter through.

1. Family doors

This one seems to be extremely common. The more deliverance you do, the more you will encounter people who have demons from their family/upbringing. Countless people I have done deliverance on got demons from being abused growing up. It's important to note that demons do not always enter because of what someone has done but often because of what someone has done to them. Physical and emotional abuse growing up is a major open door to demonic spirits. As I said earlier, this does not seem fair. A child can be demonized because of a parent or family member abusing them.

Several years ago I prayed for deliverance over a youth pastor's wife with a group of people. As she was manifesting, the demon spoke voluntarily and said, "My name is abuse. I entered into her at eight years old when her mom punched her in the face." All of us were shocked. Did the demon just casually say that? After about an hour of prayer she was fully set free by God's grace, and we asked her about that. She went on to tell us she vividly remembered the moment her mom physically abused her and all the problems she was going through now, twenty-plus years later. She felt it started when she was eight. This opened my eyes to the fact that demons can enter via trauma and abuse, even at such a young age. It's hard to believe that a lifetime of persistent issues resulted from a demonic spirit that entered her at eight years old and not even at the fault of herself but because of what her mom did.

Sadly, sexual abuse is a major open door and something that is way too common in the lives of young women and men alike. Some of the stories I've heard in deliverances make my stomach turn, and I will not even share them in this book because they are too dark and graphic. Rape, Abuse & Incest National Network (RAINN) research group revealed these startling statistics: "One in 9 girls and 1 in 20 boys under the age of 18 experience sexual abuse or assault. 82% of all victims under 18 are female. Females ages 16–19 are four times more likely than the general population to be victims of rape, attempted rape, or sexual assault. The effects of child sexual abuse can be long-lasting and affect the victim's mental health. Victims are more likely than non-victims to experience the following mental health challenges: about four times more likely to develop symptoms of drug abuse, about four times more likely to experience PTSD, and about three times more likely to experience a major depressive episode as adults."[1] These are huge numbers, and demons are using these horrific acts to demonize a large amount of the population.

Rejection from the womb is another often overlooked open door to demons. Luke 1:15 says, "He will be filled with the Holy Spirit, even before his birth." This is speaking of John the

Baptist. In deliverance ministry I would often encounter demons that would say, "I have been here since they were in their mother's womb." I thought this to be false until I thought, "Wait, if John the Baptist was filled with the Holy Spirit in his mother's womb, it doesn't seem outside the realm of possibility that a demonic spirit can enter a baby in the mother's womb." Speaking things over your unborn baby, such as "I wish I weren't pregnant," "I didn't even want this baby," "This was a mistake," "This was an accident," "I hope this baby dies," and so on can cause rejection and open your unborn baby up to demons. Research shows that babies seek love even in the womb, and when a baby is unwanted and doesn't receive that love, it becomes an open door to the spirit of rejection.

> Demons do not always enter because of what someone has done but often because of what someone else has done to them.

I prayed for a man once who had been fighting same-sex attraction. He had confessed before, "I do not want to be attracted to guys, I do not want to wear women's clothing, but something in me craves it." In his deliverance the demon said, "I've been here since he was in the womb. His parents wanted a girl, and I came because his mom constantly said, 'I don't want a boy; I want a girl.'" Somehow in the process of his mother confessing that, she gave this spirit of perversion legal right to demonize her child. I wonder how many people walk around with demons not even realizing they have been there since before they were born. Generational curses are another component of this that I will cover in a later chapter.

2. Trauma

This might feel repetitive, as I just talked about childhood trauma, but this is trauma in a more general sense. Oxford Languages (Google) defines *trauma* as "a deeply distressing or disturbing experience."[2] Demons can capitalize on traumatic events and use them as an open door to gain access to someone's life. This could be things such as traumatic surgeries, life-threatening illnesses, home break-ins, sexual trauma, attempted suicide, the loss of a loved one, near-death experiences, and violent attacks. This subject hits close to home, as my wife and I experienced a very traumatic event when my second daughter, Journey, was born.

The night of Journey's birth, everything seemed to go according to plan. It was a smooth delivery, and like most parents we couldn't have been more excited. A few hours after her birth, I got some weird stomach bug and was stuck in the bathroom, throwing up. The doctor finally came in and said to go home and that they would be fine for the night. I went home extremely sick and ended up throwing up for the next twelve hours. My cousin Jasmine, who was a night nurse off shift at the time, came and stayed with my wife, Alyssa. We did not realize that Jasmine being there would be what saved my daughter's life. In the middle of the night my wife was asleep, and Jasmine, because she was used to working the night shift, noticed that Journey had stopped breathing and was turning blue. Because Journey was born a month early, she had sleep apnea. Jasmine immediately signaled the nurses to come in, and they rushed Journey into the NICU.

They used a device that pumps air into the lungs to try to get her to start breathing again because she was completely blue from a lack of oxygen. When they did it, they pumped too much air into her lungs, and some of the air went into her chest cavity.

My wife called me, frantic, the next morning, telling me what had happened. I immediately made a post on social media asking anyone and everyone to pray for my daughter Journey. They said they would need to do surgery, but miraculously—by the power of God—she was healed and did not need surgery. She would spend the next twelve days in the NICU, but that was only due to hospital protocol.

Fast-forward a few months, and my wife was having anxiety, depression, and trouble sleeping. One night, very late, I said to Alyssa, "This isn't you; this must be something demonic going on." She instantly had a flashback and said, "Oh my goodness, I never told you, but the night Journey got rushed to the NICU, I saw a demon over my bed, and it said, 'My name is trauma, and I am going to kill your daughter.'" That was when this all started. We immediately realized all these things my wife was struggling with were a result of that demon. She went for deliverance, and all those things went away. The point of this story is to illustrate just how easily a demon can enter through trauma.

3. Occult/New Age practices

The New Age movement is growing at an alarming rate today, and I suspect this is partly a result of the modern church not demonstrating God's power. Every person has a longing for something supernatural, something spiritual, to fill the void in their life. God put this longing there, but when it is not met with the manifest presence of the Holy Spirit, people go to counterfeit versions of it. So because the modern church is not displaying the supernatural, we have an entire generation going to the New Age movement, which is the devil's counterfeit. The New Age movement and the occult both have many practices that run parallel, all of which are demonic and an open door to demons. I want to cover a few popular practices that open you up to demons, and the most popular one is yoga. Sadly, this is even practiced in many churches!

The word *yoga* means "union," and the goal is to unite one's transitory (temporary) self with the infinite Brahman, the Hindu concept of "God."[3] Does this sound Christian to you? Some people think, "Well, if I do it innocently, it will not open me up to demons. The best comparison for yoga would be the Ouija board. Yes, you can play it "just for fun" without any ill intent, but still you are participating in something that was designed to conjure spirits. The devil does not care about your intentions.

Every yoga stance represents the worship of certain Hindu gods. Your yoga teacher may bow to her class with palms together, saying, "Namaste" ("I bow to the divine in you"). This gesture done with the hands is called a mudra. According to Yoga Journal, "Mudra means 'seal,' 'gesture,' or 'mark.' Yoga mudras are symbolic gestures often practiced with the hands and fingers that facilitate the flow of energy in the subtle body and enhance one's journey within."[4]

The gesture done with palms together is known as the prayer mudra or Anjali mudra in Sanskrit. It is known as the heart seal. This is a Hindu practice that facilitates demonic activity. When you engage in this, you're inviting demons into your life. I'd rather be sealed by the Holy Spirit of God. Second Corinthians 1:21–22 (NKJV) says, "Now He who establishes us with you in Christ and has anointed us is God, who also has sealed us and given us the Spirit in our hearts as a guarantee." The Bible makes it clear that the only thing we should be sealed with is the Holy Spirit. I have dealt with many people who got demons from practicing yoga.

4. Astrology and horoscopes

These are two common practices many Christians engage in that open the door to demonic spirits. Astrology is the divination of the supposed influence of the stars and planets on human affairs and terrestrial events by their positions and aspects. A horoscope is a forecast of a person's future, typically including a delineation of character and circumstances based on the relative positions of the stars and planets at the time of that person's birth.

The question is, What's the big deal? Without a doubt, the Bible teaches that not only did God create the stars, but He also created their patterns. In Job 9:9 (NIV), we read that "[God] is the Maker of the Bear and Orion, the Pleiades and the constellations of the south." So the things that have made people curious for centuries are the stars and galaxies God created—but, He says, don't take that curiosity too far. Deuteronomy 4:19 (NIV) tells us, "And when you look up to the sky and see the sun, the moon, and the stars—all the heavenly array—do not be enticed into bowing down to them." God knew there would be a desire to bow down to these things, and that's why He gave us this warning.

To clarify, this isn't about astronomy (the scientific study of the stars) or even about God's use of the stars in His own workings and miracles, such as leading the wise men to the baby Jesus. We're talking about astrology, which is the attempt to use the stars for some hidden knowledge in a supernatural form. They do not hold that power. Look at this warning in Isaiah 47:10–15 (NIV):

> You have trusted in your wickedness....Your wisdom and knowledge mislead you....Disaster will come upon you, and you will not know how to conjure it away....Keep on, then, with your magic spells and with your many sorceries....Let your astrologers come forward, those stargazers who make predictions month by month....They are like stubble; the fire will burn them up. They cannot even save themselves....All of them go on in their error.

Do not dabble in this stuff. It is part of the occult and is very dangerous. You will open yourself up to deception and demonic spirits.

There is a very long list of things that relate to the New Age and occult that open you up to demons, but it would take far too long to list them all. Here are a few:

- visiting mediums
- Tarot cards
- voodoo
- spirit guides
- sorcery
- necromancy (communicating with the dead)
- blood oaths
- hypnosis
- palm reading
- Ouija boards
- magic books about the occult/spells
- the law of attraction
- astral projection
- channeling
- divination

All these, if you participate in them, will open you up to demonic spirits.

One of my good friends who got saved a few months after me told me that out of curiosity he played with a Ouija board at a friend's house, and a little boy in the form of a ghost followed him home that night. For two whole years up until he got saved, that ghost boy would randomly appear and follow him around. During his deliverance this demonic spirit manifested, and we were able to cast it out. From that day forward he never dealt with the spirit that was following him around. He thought the Ouija board was an innocent game, but little did he know, it was a demonic portal.

5. Sinful acts or habits

Sometimes a single act of sin can open the door to a demonic spirit, but what I have found in my experience is that it usually happens when someone makes a habit of a particular sin. First John 3:8 (ESV) says, "Whoever makes a practice of sinning is of the devil, for the devil has been sinning from the beginning. The reason the Son of God appeared was to destroy the works of the devil." Here we see the difference between sinning and practicing sin. This is when sin becomes a pattern you continue to rehearse, and like anything you practice, you get good at it. I would say you probably have made sin a practice when you're so good at it that you no longer feel guilty or remorseful. This is a breeding ground for demonic infestation. Whenever a demon speaks out of a person and declares how it got there or why it won't leave, it is usually connected to some particular sinful habit in that person's life.

Judas decided to betray Jesus, and when he left the Last Supper, the Bible says in Luke 22:3 (NIV), "Then Satan entered Judas." After that act of rebellion, Satan had a legal right to enter Judas. Judas opened a door to sin that he could not close. As I said earlier, it's not always possible to pinpoint exactly when a demon enters, but if there is a pattern of sin in a person's life, it is only a matter of time before a demon enters into them.

I can recall one deliverance where a spirit of suicide manifested in a young woman; it revealed to us voluntarily that it entered her when she was writing a suicide note. Later the girl told us she always wondered what it would be like to write a suicide note, not realizing that while she was writing, a demon of suicide entered her. Writing the note became the open door for this demon to enter.

6. Laying on of hands

You should not let just anyone lay hands on you. If you don't know their intention or spiritual history, I would politely tell them they cannot lay hands on you during prayer. Laying on of hands is a very powerful spiritual experience. Oftentimes in Scripture the Holy Spirit's power was released through the laying on of hands, but not only can the Holy Spirit's power be released— demonic spirits' power can be released as well. John Ramirez, an evangelist who is an ex-satanic high priest, told me they would always lay hands in their demonic ceremonies and practices.

Remember, the devil mimics the kingdom of God. You wouldn't drink from anyone's cup, because you don't know where their mouth has been, and in the same way you also shouldn't let anyone lay hands on you because you don't know where their hands have been. First Timothy 5:22 (NIV) says, "Do not be hasty in the laying on of hands." This is specifically talking about appointing church leadership, so I don't want to use this out of context, but I do believe there is a spiritual truth to this when it comes to praying for people as well. If you can't track someone, you shouldn't let them lay their hands on you.

7. Entertainment

Last but not least is one of the devil's favorite vehicles to access someone's life: entertainment. I mean, the first five letters are *enter*! That is something to think about. Some polls suggest that Americans spend an average of four to six hours a day being entertained on their smartphones. We are the most entertained generation in existence! The devil has definitely capitalized on that fact. I am often asked if I can get demons from watching particular shows or movies, and the answer is emphatically *yes*.

Matthew 6:22 says, "The lamp of the body is the eye. If therefore your eye is good, your whole body will be full of light. But if your eye is bad, your whole body will be full of darkness. If therefore the light that is in you is darkness, how great is that darkness!" This shows the importance of being careful what you look at. I sang a song as a kid about little eyes being careful what they see. I did not realize until I got into deliverance ministry how powerful that children's song actually is.

Years ago I was preaching in Ohio, and a woman on the church's prayer team began to manifest a demon during the altar call. This lady was on staff at the church and was supposed to help pray for people, but instead she ended up needing prayer. As the demon manifested and spoke out of her, it said, "There is no place like home; there is no place like home." Then it began to talk like characters from the old movie *The Wizard of Oz*. I was baffled by this, as the demon started quoting lines from the Tin Man and Cowardly Lion; I really didn't know what to make of this. Was this lady really manifesting some weird *Wizard of Oz* demon? I didn't stop to ask it questions. We just continued to cast it out.

Once the demon had fully left, some of the staff from the church, including the pastor who brought me out to speak, told us, "Wow! That lady is obsessed with *The Wizard of Oz*. Her house has an entire room decorated with things from the movie." She then told us that as a kid, her dad would sexually assault her, and she would rock back and forth and say, "There's no place like home; there's no place like home." That movie somehow became a part of her trauma and opened her up to some bizarre demons I had never encountered before. To this day I don't fully understand this situation, but I can confidently tell you it was *real*.

I would also like to emphasize that not only do movies and television shows give demons access, but so does music. Music is far more powerful than people are willing to admit. Many people believe Satan was in charge of the music in heaven, although this is not specifically made clear in Scripture. What is clear is that Satan uses music today to further his agenda. This is a common belief because the second part of Ezekiel 28:13 (NKJV) says this about Satan: "The workmanship of your timbrels and pipes was prepared for you on the day you were created." Speaking through the prophet Ezekiel, God said that Satan has musical instruments in his body. Today some of his most powerful servants are musicians on the *Billboard* charts. Everyone knows hearing a song can take you back. There is spiritual power in music. All music glorifies something. If it's not glorifying God, who is it glorifying?

Many Christian leaders say it's fine to listen to worldly music. I don't see gray areas; there is a kingdom of light and a kingdom of darkness and no middle kingdom. One of the first things I did when I got saved was delete the forty thousand songs I had on my iTunes. I knew the power of music.

There is a reason that ten thousand young people will go to a rave and dance to the same beat for six hours, and the genre is called trance. I'm sorry if you don't think there is power in it. You are sadly mistaken.

The seven open doors I listed here are obviously not all of them, but I wanted to pinpoint the most common ones I see when doing deliverance. If we can remain vigilant to keep doors closed, we can live our lives demon-proof. I would like to end this chapter by leading you in a prayer to close any doors that might be open. Repeat this:

> *Lord, I come before You and ask that You would reveal any doors in my life that are open; I choose today to shut every door that is open to the enemy in my life.*

Satan, I command you and your demons to leave immediately; you have no power or authority over me. I am a child of the most high God. Jesus, help me close these doors today and leave them closed once and for all! Help me, Lord, not to make sin a practice; cover me with Your mercy, grace, and blood. Thank You, Lord, for hearing my prayer. In Jesus' name, amen!

I want you to go right now and get rid of anything in your life that is an open door to demons, slam that door shut, and choose never to open it again!

Chapter 5
EIGHT SIGNS YOU MIGHT HAVE A DEMON

ONE OF THE greatest tactics of the devil, if not the greatest tactic, is convincing the world he does not exist. I've heard people say, "Well, if the devil was real, why wouldn't he show up at the national football halftime show and let the world know how real he is." It is straightforward: If people understood how real he was, they would try to resist him! The more he can hide, and the more he can remain undetected, the better off he is.

Think about it: If you knew a demon was living inside you, you would probably do anything you could to seek out freedom. A person who doesn't realize a demon is hiding in them will never seek out deliverance but instead convince themselves they will always be this way. This is exactly what the demons want: to continue to live inside you without any resistance. In the same way a doctor will ask you what your symptoms are when you come in saying you're sick, we can look at common symptoms of demonization to see if a demon is hiding. I have dealt with people over and over who had demons for decades and had no clue something was there hiding for that long. I can't stress enough how good demons are at hiding.

THE POTENCY OF CAMOUFLAGE

Demons are professionals at hiding and remaining undetected. They use a war tactic called camouflage. Google defines *camouflage* as "to hide or disguise the presence of (a person, animal, or object) by means of camouflage."[1] It is a potent weapon that almost every army in the world uses to gain an advantage over their enemy. If an army can remain undetected, they have the element of surprise when attacking. Not only do they have the element of surprise as an offensive strategy, but they are also extremely hard to fight against because you can't see them and don't know they are there.

How can we fight an enemy we are unaware of? That is the point of this chapter—to make you aware of a demon hiding in you or a demon hiding in the person you plan to pray deliverance prayer over. If you can bring the demon into the light and expose it, you have a massive advantage over it! After all, 1 Thessalonians 5:5 (NKJV) says, "You are all sons of light and sons of the day. We are not of the night nor of darkness." As God's children and ambassadors we don't hide our plans because we live in the light; we don't need to work in darkness like the devil and his demons. Instead, we expose the darkness! The moment demons are brought to the light, they lose their power.

When a person manifests a demon during deliverance prayer—meaning the demon surfaces by growling and speaking through the person, the person's heart begins to race, a voice starts to talk to them, and so on—the first thing the person usually says is, "Wow, I didn't even know I had a demon!" I can't count how many times I've heard that. It is a testament to how good demons are at hiding. I have found that demons will resist manifesting as much as possible. They don't want their victims to know they are there. Like a squatter living in a house rent-free, they want to remain unseen.

Demons are opportunists and only expose themselves when they absolutely have to. I have noticed that during anointed preaching or in an anointed environment such as worship, at times they have no choice but to surface. These environments can be good atmospheres to kick-start a deliverance. My rule of thumb is if a person manifests and you have the ability to pray deliverance over them, do it right then because the demon may not manifest itself like that again. It is usually easier to do deliverance when the manifestation is already happening than trying to get a demon to manifest and come out from hiding.

This is what demons do; they hide until the most opportune time for an attack. Usually, they do not harass or attack constantly, as that would give away their position, but instead, they wait until moments of weakness or when they can do maximum damage to your life. For example, a demon of lust might remain dormant for years, and you may think, "Well, I must be free!" Now you're happily married, and a few years into the marriage, that demon manifests itself

> Demons will resist manifesting as much as possible. Like a squatter living in a house rent-free, they want to remain unseen.

and begins wreaking havoc in your marriage. Meanwhile, you thought that entire time you were free but did not realize the demon was hiding and waiting to attack.

A spirit of suicide might live inside someone for years and wait until they lose a job, go through a bad breakup, or have a life-altering event. When the demon sees that person is at their weakest, it will pounce. Even though that demon has lived inside the person for years, it waited for the most opportune time to attack. We need to be on the offensive, not the defensive. We cannot wait for a demon to attack us before we go through deliverance; we need to attack it before it can wreak havoc on our lives. It is heartbreaking how many people live in bondage and have no clue simply because nobody has told them that what they're going through might be a result of a demonic spirit.

OUT FROM HIDING

I remember doing a deliverance conference in Texas, and a woman walked up to me and asked how she could know if she had a demon. As we talked more and more about deliverance, she began to manifest a demon: She started to sweat, her heart raced, and she said a voice told her to get away from me and not talk to me anymore. She cried and said, "I can't believe I have a demon, and I'm manifesting right now. This is terrible!"

I told her, "No, this is actually amazing."

"What do you mean?" she said. "Why would this be amazing?"

"Because for years this demon has been hiding in you, but now that you know it's there, we can deal with it and cast it out."

The look on her face was one of relief, as if to say, "Wow, I didn't even think of that."

If we can help people see there is a demon there, that's the first step in getting them free. Our goal is not to get people to manifest. It's to get them free! Sometimes the manifestation is inevitable, and in that moment you can assure them this is not a bad thing.

In the past decade I've watched the devil do everything in his power to keep the church ignorant—perhaps the greatest weapon he uses to keep us from fighting against him. You know what they say: Ignorance is bliss is only said by the ignorant. I know what you're thinking: "Isaiah, I can't believe you're calling the church ignorant." But *ignorant* does not mean stupid; the definition of *ignorant* is lacking knowledge or information. You don't know what you don't know! This is why I believe this book is so crucial: You're finally getting information that for years you did not know.

Knowledge is power! Hosea 4:6 (NKJV) says, "My people are destroyed for lack of knowledge." This is a powerful verse; the reason for their destruction was that they did not know something God wanted them to know. Demons love when we don't believe they exist. They love when we are clueless about deliverance and tell people not to worry about casting out demons. The truth is they love keeping you ignorant of their strategies. Demons love when you think there is no path to freedom and you will always live in fear, anxiety, addiction, depression—and the list goes on. I'm telling you right now you can be free from these things in Jesus' name! It is time to come out of ignorance and start exposing the devil's plans.

Not Everything Is a Demon

Before discussing signs that you might have a demon hiding, I want to make sure we don't think *everything* is a demon. I've often been accused of thinking everything is a demon, to which I reply, "I don't think everything is a demon, but you don't think anything is a demon!" There is a danger in both ways of thinking. We don't want to live thinking everything is a demon and be paranoid, but we also don't want to live thinking nothing is a demon and give the devil free rein to do what he wants unchallenged.

It's vital that you know you can't crucify a demon and you can't cast out the flesh. What I mean by that is if something is the flesh, we must crucify it; but if something is a demon, we must cast it out. Jesus taught both things. He taught that we must crucify our flesh, and He also taught that must cast out demons. Most people do not fully understand the difference between the flesh and a demon (they are not the same thing), so let me briefly, in the most basic sense, describe what the flesh is.

Understanding the Flesh

In the Bible "the flesh" refers to our fallen human nature, characterized by sinful tendencies and desires. Romans 7:18–20 (NKJV) states,

> For I know that in me (that is, in my flesh) nothing good dwells; for to will is present with me, but how to perform what is good I do not find. For the good that I will to do, I do not do; but the evil I will not to do, that I practice. Now if I do what I will not to do, it is no longer I who do it, but sin that dwells in me.

This is the apostle Paul describing that sinful nature we all battle with before coming to Christ. This is the part of you that is an enemy to God; it entices us and drags us away from God. This sinful nature cannot be cast out. It must be crucified. Prayer, fasting, and spending time in God's Word are simple yet effective ways to crucify your flesh. Before you think you will always struggle with the flesh and your sinful desires, let me share some good news with you. The good news is that through Christ we can overcome the power of the flesh.

Romans 6:6–7 (NIV) says, "For we know that our old self was crucified with him so that the body ruled by sin might be done away with, that we should no longer be slaves to sin—because anyone who has died has been set free from sin."

Notice Paul says we should no longer be slaves to sin; there are

Christians who still are, but they shouldn't be! It is not God's desire that we remain a slave to our fleshly desires after being born again. Will we still fight temptation? Yes. Will we still need to crucify our flesh from time to time? Yes. But remember, we are no longer slaves. Demons do give us ungodly desires, but don't automatically think that because you have an ungodly desire it's a demon, because sometimes it is the flesh.

Our fleshly desires often lead us astray, tempt us to sin and disobey God and do things we know we should not be doing as children of God. Look at what Galatians 5:19–21 (NKJV) says:

> Now the works of the flesh are evident, which are: adultery, fornication, uncleanness, lewdness, idolatry, sorcery, hatred, contentions, jealousies, outbursts of wrath, selfish ambitions, dissensions, heresies, envy, murders, drunkenness, revelries, and the like; of which I tell you beforehand, just as I also told you in time past, that those who practice such things will not inherit the kingdom of God.

Interestingly, Paul does not say these are the works of demons even though demons can definitely tempt you to do these things; he says they are works of the flesh. I'm trying to make it very clear to you that some things are of the flesh and not always demons. I believe demons exaggerate the flesh, work with the flesh, and go hand in hand with the flesh to cause you to sin.

If something is the flesh, we must crucify it, but if something is a demon, we must cast it out.

It's also true that not every temptation comes from a demon. Sometimes the flesh will tempt us. If you're tempted, it does not mean you automatically have a demon. Look at what

James 1:14–15 says: "Temptation comes from our own desires, which entice us and drag us away. These desires give birth to sinful actions. And when sin is allowed to grow, it gives birth to death."

So first our temptation comes from our own desires—that is, our own flesh. This is not to say demons can't tempt you, because they can, but my point is that the flesh also tempts you, according to James.

Second, these desires entice us and drag us away. Sin and temptation will take you to places you do not want to go! There is an enticing power to the flesh that we must crucify and resist when we feel it.

Third, these desires give birth to sinful actions. If you let these desires in you fester and grow, they have a baby named sinful actions. Now not only are you tempted, but you have started giving in to that temptation.

Fourth, if sin is allowed to grow, it gives birth to death. Death means separation from God. What James is saying is *Do not let sin grow!* Cut it at the root. The more you sin, the easier it will be to continue. You must uproot it at infancy, before it grows into maturity and destroys your life.

Now that we have a better understanding of the flesh, you might ask, "OK, so how do I know if I have a demon or am just battling the flesh?" To be honest, it's not always easy, but here is the easiest way to tell: The flesh does not talk to you. The flesh will not speak to you in your mind. Demons are persons without bodies. The flesh is a part of you. If someone is talking to you in your head, that is *not* the flesh. That is a demon! If you hear a voice in your head saying, "You should cut your arm. It will make you feel better," or, "Everyone would be happier if you ended your life," or, "You're worthless; nobody loves you," those are demons speaking to you that are living inside you and must be cast out.

If a thought that is destructive in nature randomly pops into your head, that is likely a demon, not your flesh. It is not normal to have thoughts in your head and then another voice speaking to you, telling you dark and destructive things. Sadly, we have made hearing voices normal when it is not. The only voice I want to hear is the voice of the Holy Spirit. I think it's time we made hearing the voice of God normal and hearing the voice of demons abnormal.

Eight Signs You Might Have a Demon

Now that we understand how demons love to hide, that not everything is a demon but some things are the flesh, and how to know the difference, let's discuss eight signs you might have a demon hiding. After all, that is the name of the chapter.

1. Manifesting a demon

If you manifest a demon, meaning a demon surfaces, you know right away a demon is there, and you can now deal with it.

Some manifestations might include a demon starting to laugh out of the person being delivered, demons speaking out, saying, "How did you know I am here?," demons making the person slither like a snake or do abnormal body contortions, hysterical laughing or crying, growling or making animal noises, a racing heartbeat, sweating profusely when talking about deliverance or receiving deliverance prayer, feeling extremely nervous when talking about deliverance—the list is long, but these are some main manifestations. In all honesty, I would not consider manifesting a sign that a demon *might* be hiding, because if you manifest, the demon is no longer hiding. It is out in the open.

In Mark 1 Jesus is preaching His first sermon in a synagogue, and as He's preaching, a demon manifests in a man. Look at what happens:

> Suddenly, a man in the synagogue who was possessed by an
> evil spirit cried out, "Why are you interfering with us, Jesus of
> Nazareth? Have you come to destroy us? I know who you are—
> the Holy One of God!"
>
> —Mark 1:23

Notice it says the man cried out, but it wasn't the man speaking.
It was the evil spirit. Also, it's interesting that the demon says
"us" multiple times, revealing that there are multiple demons in
the man. Now we don't have to guess if this man might have a
demon because he is clearly manifesting by a demon speaking
out of him. We know he has demons and needs deliverance.
Thankfully, Jesus, unlike most Christians today, did not leave the
man demonized but commanded the demon to leave the man.

Mark 1:25–26 says,

> But Jesus reprimanded him. "Be quiet! Come out of the
> man," he ordered. At that, the evil spirit screamed, threw the
> man into a convulsion, and then came out of him.

Notice how it says the evil spirit screamed (manifested) and
threw the man into convulsions (manifested) and then came out.
This is common in deliverance, where you will see a dramatic
manifestation before the demon leaves. Let me give you this last
warning before I go into other signs you might have a demon
hiding in you. Just because you have one or some of these signs
does not mean you have a demon hiding. It's just likely you do.
This is not a 100 percent, guaranteed way to know, but it will
help unmask and expose hiding demons.

2. Dominating/intrusive thoughts

These are thoughts you did not create, the Holy Spirit did not
give you, and that are extremely hard to get rid of. They also usually come at unconventional times and without reason. I've had

the most normal people you can imagine say, "I had a random thought that I should kill my wife [or my kid]. I would never in a million years do that, but this thought was so overwhelming!"

In 2010 before I was delivered, I remember sitting down to eat breakfast one day and getting the most twisted and perverted thoughts. I knew it wasn't me but didn't know what it was. I know now it was a demon, but sadly, at the time, I thought it was just normal. In early 2011 I was delivered, and to this day I've never had thoughts like that. Likely, you know exactly what I mean when I say these thoughts are dominating. They feel as though they suffocate you and don't let you up for air.

How many people walk around suffering in silence, thinking it's normal to have thoughts like this? Only after you receive deliverance will you realize it is not normal! The devil dominates the mind; God renews the mind. If you feel your mind being dominated, that is a demon, not God. One thing I hear from people over and over after they get deliverance is, "My mind feels so empty! I was so used to hearing demons talk all day and getting thoughts from demons all day, and I didn't even realize it until now."

This sign really hits home for me because of something that happened about a month before my salvation experience in December 2010. I was at a hotel party, and there were fifteen or twenty of us drinking and listening to music, as we usually did. At about 1 a.m., the party ended and my girlfriend and I, who were living in a sinful relationship, went to bed. At about 2 a.m. I couldn't sleep, and something happened to me that had never happened before. I got this overwhelming thought that I should jump off the balcony. It's important you know I have never, even before I was saved, had the desire to take my life. I was not suicidal whatsoever, but I just could not shake this thought. This thought dominated me for what felt like an hour, but in reality it was only a few minutes.

It got so bad that I got out of bed, went onto the balcony, and looked over as if I were going to do it. In the middle of this experience, what I know now as a demon telling me to kill myself, another thought told me, "Go lie down! Go to bed! Go lie down!" By the grace of God I went to bed, and my life was spared. Little did I know that a month later I would get radically saved, on January 12, 2011. I look back and realize that was the devil's last-ditch effort to kill me before I got saved. Praise God for His saving power even when I wasn't serving Him. The point of sharing that story is to show you how powerful these thoughts can be.

3. Voices in your head

This is a dead giveaway. If you have a voice speaking to you, saying things like "us," "we," "Let's go do this," "We should say this," and so forth, that is a demon talking to you. If a voice says, "I am going to do this to you," that is a demon talking. A girl I recently interviewed on my podcast who shared her deliverance story told me every time she would walk into a room with people in it, voices in her head would say, "They hate you. Nobody here likes you. Nobody wants you here. You're ugly," and so on. These voices would say all kinds of foul things to her and about her. She convinced herself it was her own thoughts, but after going through deliverance, she realized those were demons talking to her the entire time.

Only two voices can speak to our minds: the Holy Spirit's and demons'. It's obvious that the Holy Spirit would never say those things, so we can easily conclude that they were demons. Often demons will blaspheme God or say sinful things about God. I was once doing deliverance training in North Carolina, and the pastor's wife came up to me afterward and said, "I've never told anyone, but every time my husband is preaching, I hear a voice saying curse words in my head!" By the grace of God, she got delivered that day, and she has updated me since that she no longer hears curse words during sermons.

I heard a pastor once preach, saying it's normal to hear voices in your head. It made me so sad that he was teaching thousands of people that hearing from demons is normal. Instead of teaching people that hearing from demons is normal, let's teach them that deliverance is normal!

4. Hatred toward others for no apparent reason

If you're experiencing hatred toward a specific race, parents, friends, church leaders, authority figures such as police officers, and so forth, this is likely demonic. Before I went through deliverance, I was racist toward my *own* race! How twisted is that, to be racist against yourself, yet that is exactly how demons manipulated and deceived me. Demons love to breed hatred into the hearts of humans to try to divide and conquer us. Listen to Matthew 12:25–26 (NKJV):

> But Jesus knew their thoughts, and said to them: "Every kingdom divided against itself is brought to desolation, and every city or house divided against itself will not stand. If Satan casts out Satan, he is divided against himself. How then will his kingdom stand?"

The purpose of the devil making you hate your fellow brother is to cause division. It amazes me how many Christians hate deliverance ministers for no reason. Well, there is a reason: The demons are causing them to hate ministries that destroy Satan's kingdom. The theme I hope you're picking up is "without reason."

5. Physical symptoms that have no medical reasoning

Demons are often the cause of sickness and disease, and one of the dead giveaways of sickness being caused by a demon is when doctors have no explanation for it. Many people come to me and say, "I have a specific pain in my body, and I've been to every doctor, and everything checks out. I'm healthy." This is a telltale sign that a demon may be causing that specific sickness or pain. Luke 13:10–13 (NKJV) is a perfect example of this.

> Now He was teaching in one of the synagogues on the Sabbath. And behold, there was a woman who had a spirit of infirmity eighteen years, and was bent over and could in no way raise herself up. But when Jesus saw her, He called her to Him and said to her, "Woman, you are loosed from your infirmity." And He laid His hands on her, and immediately she was made straight, and glorified God.

This woman was severely crippled, not from a natural sickness that doctors could diagnose but from a demonic spirit. Jesus did not say to go see a doctor. Jesus loosed her from her infirmity, and immediately her back was straight. How incredible is it that what doctors couldn't do in a lifetime, Jesus did in a moment!

I had a good friend whose little sister was extremely sick all the time, and doctors could not help her. One day we went to her house to pray for her, and the Holy Spirit told me she didn't need healing. She needed deliverance. Sure enough, as we began to pray and command the spirit of infirmity out of her, there was a dramatic manifestation and then freedom. After this deliverance she never had those symptoms of sickness again.

It is so vital we listen to the Holy Spirit, because sometimes we try to pray for healing when really we should be praying for deliverance. Often in the New Testament you will see that when Jesus prayed for the sick, He also cast out demons. In fact, Matthew 8:16–17 (ESV) says,

> That evening they brought to him many who were oppressed by demons, and he cast out the spirits with a word and healed all who were sick. This was to fulfill what was spoken by the prophet Isaiah: "He took our illnesses and bore our diseases."

We see here Jesus healing the sick and casting out demons. So it's not one or the other; it's both!

6. Recurring nightmares/night terrors

Demons love to attack at night—it is when we are most vulnerable to spiritual attack. Although our bodies are asleep, our spirits do not sleep, and demons take advantage of this fact. You might wake up feeling a weight on your chest, not be able to speak the name of Jesus, see a dark figure at the foot of your bed or corner of your room, or have the feeling of being suffocated. People who are demonized seem to be much more prone to being attacked by demons in their sleep.

If someone is having nonstop nightmares, I always recommend they seek out deliverance. The word *nightmare* is derived from the Old English *mare*, a mythological demon or goblin who torments others with frightening dreams. Even the worldly definition of the word describes a demonic being. A helpful tip is to pray for the armor of God before bed. I make it a nightly thing before bed to pray the full armor of God. It is very important you be

> Demons are often the cause of sickness and disease, and one of the dead giveaways is when doctors have no explanation for it.

careful what you watch before bed, as watching horror movies, crime documentaries, and shows like that make you extremely susceptible to demonic attack. Here is a scripture I like to quote before bed if I am dealing with attacks at night: "Do not be afraid of the terrors of the night, nor the arrow that flies in the day" (Ps. 91:5). The same God who protects you in the day will also protect you at night.

7. Mental illnesses

This is a very controversial one, and let me be the first to say I do not believe every mental illness is demonic, but I believe some are. Put it this way: If you go to a doctor and say, "I hear voices," or "I have multiple personalities," they're not going to say, "You have a demon. Go get deliverance." They are likely going to diagnose you with a mental illness and put you on medication. This is a huge issue and sad reality that I could probably write an entire book on. Let me give you an example.

According to the National Institute of Mental Health, this is a main symptom of schizophrenia: "Hallucinations: When a person sees, hears, smells, tastes, or feels things that are not actually there. Hearing voices is common for people with schizophrenia. People who hear voices may hear them for a long time before family or friends notice a problem."[2] So they say hearing voices is a main symptom, yet we know that is also a main symptom of demonization. Do you see how these two things cross paths? If you begin to look into many mental illnesses today, you will see demons are responsible for not all but some of them. You might say, "Well, Isaiah, I have a mental illness, but it's not a demon. Is there hope for me?" Yes, because we serve a God who heals and delivers! I rest my point. The rabbit hole on this goes deep; just know that oftentimes mental illness is a sign of a demon.

8. Irrational fears and phobias

This is a major sign that a demon is hiding, especially when you have fears that are irrational in nature. I've dealt with people who are deathly afraid of harmless animals. One woman we did deliverance on was terrified of birds; I mean, if she saw a bird, she would go into a full panic. She had no clue why she was like this, but during her deliverance an ancient bird spirit manifested to the point she was making bird noises. This might sound crazy to you, but for her it was very real. After her deliverance, that phobia of birds completely left her.

Many people suffer from fear in the car; they constantly think they're going to wreck or die in a car accident. It's so crippling they often avoid freeways or driving in general because getting in a car gives them a panic attack. I have met many of these people and seen how life-changing deliverance was for them. The Bible clarifies that fear is a spirit; 2 Timothy 1:7 (NKJV) says, "For God has not given us a spirit of fear, but of power and of love and of a sound mind." So fear is a spirit that does not come from God; it must come from Satan. He is the author of fear and torment. God's desire for our life is that we would walk in power and love, not fear and dread. If you or someone you know is dealing with an irrational fear or phobia, it's likely from a demon.

There are so many different signs you may have a demon hiding, but these are the most common, in my opinion.

Here are several other signs you have a demon, but this is by no means exhaustive:

- Eating and sleeping disorders

- Dark countenance/hollow look

- Constantly challenging God's Word

- Uncontrollable anger

- Desire to be unclean

- Suddenly tired when reading or praying

- Talking to inanimate objects

- Feeling stuck in the wrong body

- Confusion and lack of time perception

- Obsession with witchcraft/occult

- Perverted sexual desires

In the next chapter we'll turn our attention to cursed items that invite demons into your home, with or without your knowledge—and how you can keep it clear of demonic infestation.

Chapter 6
CURSED ITEMS THAT INVITE DEMONS INTO YOUR HOME

O NE OF THE worst things a family can experience is a home break-in. Most people have a sense of safety and security in their homes, and when that feeling is broken, it's a horrible and often traumatizing experience. On July 10, 1996, when my wife was four years old, she was having a sleepover with some of her cousins, and in the middle of the night a man broke into her family home. As he was stealing the family TV in the living room, her dad went out to try to fight him off. Because it was so dark, her dad did not realize the man had a knife, and during the confrontation the intruder stabbed him multiple times. My wife and her cousins came out and saw this confrontation taking place, which traumatized her as a young child.

After her dad and this man fought back and forth for a while, finally the man ran out the door, and it was then her dad realized he had been stabbed. He was rushed to the hospital, where the doctors said if it was not for his gut, the knife would have punctured his organs, and he would be dead. To this day my wife makes sure every night that all our doors are locked and our alarm is set.

The threat of home invasions is real, but what if I told you burglars are not the only ones breaking into homes. You see, the truth is there is a much worse enemy and a more common break-in, and demonic spirits carry it out. Principally, demons crave a body to live in (preferably human bodies), but they also make it their goal to enter into our physical homes and wreak havoc. We may be good at protecting our house from physical intruders, but what about spiritual intruders?

Demons are spiritual burglars that seek to steal, kill, and destroy. I have four young daughters, so without a doubt if I heard a noise at night and noticed someone breaking into my home, I would grab my shotgun and do whatever I needed to protect my family. As the man of the house, I would not ask my wife to get up and see what the noise was. I would take that responsibility, and I think most men reading this would do the same thing.

But what happens when spiritual intruders try to enter our home? Sadly, most parents are not this serious when it comes to spiritual intruders. Most people would not own a house without locks, yet many of us have no spiritual locks in our homes. Having no safeguards and no barriers leaves our homes vulnerable to demonic intrusion.

Looking back to the Garden of Eden, one of Adams' original jobs was protecting it. Genesis 2:15 (NKJV) says, "Then the LORD God took the man and put him in the garden of Eden to tend and keep it." The word *keep* in Hebrew is *shamar*, and it is translated to mean keep, watch over, guard, and defend.[1] Why would God tell Adam to protect the place he lived? Because God knew there would be intruders, and we find out later there was indeed an intruder whose name was Satan. In the same way, our homes are our gardens that we are called to protect to keep the devil's agents—demons—from entering.

If the devil could invade Adam's home, which was perfect and without sin, how easy do you think it is for him to invade ours? God gave Adam authority to take dominion over the animals. Adam had the right to tell the snake to leave, yet he did not exercise his authority over the devil. We also have authority over demonic spirits, yet we never exercise that right when it comes to our homes.

Having a security system in your home will help you protect yourself from intruders, but it will not make the intruders leave. *Forbes* did a study on home break-ins and said, "On average, 3,062 burglaries happen in the U.S. every day, 72% of reported burglaries happened when nobody was at home, homes without security systems are 300% more likely to be robbed, but only 25% of Americans have a home security system."[2] So clearly, security systems prevent break-ins, but sadly, most people do not have them.

> Most people would not own a house without locks, yet many of us have no spiritual locks in our homes.

The Holy Spirit is like a spiritual security system that can warn us of intruders, but it is our job to fight against those intruders. Do not ignore the warnings of the Holy Spirit when He tells you something is trying to get in. When He is sounding the alarm, pay attention. This might be something as simple as Him telling you your kids are watching something they shouldn't be watching or engaging in relationships they shouldn't be involved in. Maybe He is convicting you of a wrong practice you are doing that is opening the door to demonic spirits.

In this chapter I will outline specific items that open up your home to demonic spirits and actually attract them. You can have the best security system in the world, but it won't help if you always leave doors open. We must lock every door to ensure nothing gets into our home uninvited.

Demons dwelling in houses is not a new phenomenon but has been occurring for a very long time. Even the secular world recognizes these spirits by their name, *poltergeists*, which comprises the German word *polter*, meaning noisy, and *geist*, which means spirit or ghost.[3] In my years of doing deliverance ministry, I have had many requests to visit homes to pray these things out of people's houses. I've heard things such as doors slamming, footsteps at night, dark figures walking around the house, and so on. One woman even told me that all the Bibles in her house would be moved around and hidden every night!

This raises the question "Can demons really dwell in houses or specific physical locations?" The answer is quite simple: A demonic spirit can live anywhere it is welcome or allowed to assume authority without being hindered. Revelation 2:13 (NIV), in the letter to the church in Pergamum, says, "I know where you live—where Satan has his throne." This was a physical dwelling place where Satan was residing. So if Satan can dwell in physical spaces, it only makes sense that his demons can as well.

Sometimes the disturbances these demons cause are so bad that people will move out of their homes. I want to equip you so you won't have to move out of your house if there are demons there; instead, they will have to move out. We don't move out for demons; demons move out for us! They gain access to a home in the same way they gain access to live in a person: through a legal right. Usually, in the case of your home, it's an item in your possession. If you have any of the items I am about to list, get rid of them immediately.

Accursed items

Plainly put, these are items God told you to get rid of or items you know you should not have. These may not be the same for everyone. If the Holy Spirit told you to get rid of it and you don't, that item becomes accursed. The moment I got saved, the Holy Spirit convicted me and told me to get rid of my ungodly music, ungodly movies, and video games. I was heavily addicted to all three. What has God told you to remove? What has the Holy Spirit convicted you of that you disobeyed? Maybe He has told you to get rid of those horror movies; maybe He has told you to pour that alcohol down the drain; maybe He has told you to throw out that vape. Whatever it is, obedience is better than sacrifice, so get rid of it now.

Look at what Deuteronomy 7:25–26 says:

> You must burn their idols in fire, and you must not covet the silver or gold that covers them. You must not take it, or it will become a trap to you, for it is detestable to the LORD your God. Do not bring any detestable objects into your home, for then you will be destroyed, just like them. You must utterly detest such things, for they are set apart for destruction.

When you take accursed things that God has said to destroy, you come under a curse. Notice how the scripture says not to take them into your home, or you will be destroyed. This is a pretty stern warning that still applies to us today. Televisions have become modern-day idols, smartphones have become modern-day idols, and the various forms of entertainment have become modern-day idols. We must be careful about what we allow in our homes. The word *accursed* is the Hebrew word *cherem*, and one of its meanings is something "devoted to destruction."[4] In the previous passage, something God said to destroy did not get destroyed.

In Joshua 7 we see this play out in the life of a man named Achan. He stole things that were to be devoted to God, and a curse came on him, his family, and all the camp of Israel. Their enemies were easily able to defeat them because there was a curse on them due to Achan's actions. I wonder how many defeats we have experienced because we've kept what God said to destroy. For that curse to be removed, they had to destroy the items and kill Achan and his entire family under the Law of Moses. Thank God we are not under the Law of Moses to that capacity, but we still need to destroy the things God says to destroy. In fact, this is exactly what the new converts did in the Book of Acts.

> We don't move out for demons; demons move out for us!

Acts 19:18–19 says, "Many who became believers confessed their sinful practices. A number of them who had been practicing sorcery brought their incantation books and burned them at a public bonfire. The value of the books was several million dollars." A revival so powerful was taking place that these pagans were willing to burn several million dollars' worth of their demonic items!

My eyes became open to the idea that demons can be attracted or invited through certain items during a deliverance. I was with a team of people praying for a girl who started manifesting a demon during a prayer meeting. About thirty minutes into praying deliverance for this girl, the demon, who would not leave, said, "I don't even want to be here. They brought me here in the airplane across the world, and I didn't even want to come!"

We were all completely stunned, not understanding what the demon was talking about. Then it said, "I am attached to the plate." We still did not know what the demon was talking about or what to make of this, so we continued to pray. After about another hour, the deliverance was done, and we felt as if she was free. We asked her if she had any idea what this demon was talking about, and she said, "Oh my gosh, yes!" She said a missionary friend had brought her a plate from Africa that was a home decorative piece. She said, "I have it on a shelf on display right now!" We told her to get rid of it when she got home because a demon was somehow attached to this item.

The story gets even weirder. When she got home, she called us and said the plate was knocked off the shelf and shattered on the ground. This story still makes me scratch my head, but ever since this situation I tell people to be extremely careful about items they bring from other countries. I do believe demons can attach to items and even enter our homes through them.

Crystals

Healing crystals have become a booming trend, and many people use them to attract finances, health, prosperity, and many other things. This is a New Age practice that is extremely dangerous, as it attracts and invites demons. We do not look to creation for healing, peace, prosperity, or power. We look to the Creator. When we idolize and worship creation, we open ourselves up to demonic attack. People justify using these occult items by saying, "Well, God created them. Why wouldn't He want me to use them?"

Yes, God created them, but He did not say to worship them or use them to seek healing. Humanity has a long history of worshipping God's creation rather than Him. Crystals certainly are beautiful objects, for God created them. Revelation 21 even tells us that portions of God's glorious heavenly city, the New Jerusalem, will be constructed from crystal.

Bibleinfo.com has a great article on this topic that I want to highlight.

> When evaluating the appropriateness of using crystals for healing purposes, it is important to be aware of the fact that the majority of experts who promote crystal healing are involved in the occult. The word occult means "hidden." Occultism concerns itself with the study and utilization of supernatural influences, powers, and phenomena that are normally hidden from the regular physical senses and are generally considered to be outside the realm of traditional scientific observation. Occultists believe that human beings and the world in which we live are permeated by invisible mystical energies. They believe that these energies can be focused and directed by "sacred stones," such as crystals and other talismans, so as to induce physical healing and spiritual enlightenment. In addition to involvement with crystal power, occultism is associated with other mystical practices such as astrology, numerology, divination, tarot cards, psychic healing, mediumship, spirit channeling, Eastern religions, ritual magic, and sorcery.[5]

What does God say about involvement with the occult? He warned the Israelites against it when they were about to enter the Promised Land of Canaan.

> When you enter the land the LORD your God is giving you, do not learn to imitate the detestable ways of the nations there. Let no one be found among you who practices divination or sorcery, interprets omens, engages in witchcraft, or casts spells, or who is a medium or spiritist or who consults the dead. Anyone who does these things is detestable to the LORD.
> —DEUTERONOMY 18:9–12, NIV

The use of "sacred stones" for mystical purposes was common among the pagan peoples of the Bible lands. Called amulets, these magical charms were made in the form of small pendants attached to a necklace or bracelet. They were worn to protect a person from negative energies, evil, and injury, and also to bring good luck. God uttered a stern warning to the false prophetesses of Israel, who, in their apostasy, had adopted the pagan practice of wearing amulets.

This is what the sovereign Lord says:

> Woe to the women who sew magic charms on all their wrists and make veils of various lengths for their heads in order to ensnare people. Will you ensnare the lives of my people but preserve your own? I am against your magic charms with which you ensnare people like birds, and I will tear them from your arms; I will set free the people that you ensnare like birds. I will tear off your veils and save my people from your hands, and they will no longer fall prey to your power.
> —Ezekiel 13:18, 20–21, NIV

The article I just referenced (Bibleinfo.com) has so much good information, but I think it's clear that as Christians we should not have any involvement with healing crystals of any kind. If you have any in your home that you're using to attract some energy, get rid of them immediately, as they attract demons.

Tarot and angel cards

I have been alarmed to see these occult cards spreading through Christian communities. Recently I was preaching at my home church, and a group of people came and handed out angel cards. The crazy part is that they actually did not see anything wrong with it. I told the security team to kindly let them know they were not allowed to do that, and they apologized. It shocked me that people in church would think these things are OK.

Tarot cards are heavily used in the occult. The term *occult* originates from the Latin *occultus*, signifying the concealment or secrecy of certain aspects. In satanism, witchcraft, and ritual magic, the term implies practices to attain insights into the spiritual realm or to wield power through interactions with spirits of the dead, pagan deities, and so-called "spirit guides." In biblical terms this entails communication with fallen angels, commonly called demons or familiar spirits.

The origins of tarot is a subject of debate among both tarot historians and practicing psychics. However, it appears to have originated as a card game in the fourteenth century, gradually transforming into a tool for divination. Two renowned French occultists are often acknowledged for their roles in popularizing tarot card readings in Paris during the 1800s. Since then, tarot reading has become a specialized skill that is commonly used today for psychic readings.

While some stick to tarot cards alone, others also use oracle cards and angel cards for different reasons. The first tarot deck designed specifically for occult purposes was created in 1789. These occult decks consist of seventy-eight cards divided into two "arcana." These and the cards specific to them are the Major Arcana: Cards in this part include the Emperor, the Empress, the High Priestess, the Magician, the Hierophant, the Hermit, Temperance, the Tower, the Chariot, Strength, Justice, the Lovers, the Moon, the Star, the Sun, the World, Wheel of Fortune, the Hanged Man, the Devil, Death, the Fool, and Judgment.

Nothing about this practice or these cards is Christian. They are purely demonic and used for divination purposes, which the Bible detests. Every tarot card reader has their own method of reading the cards, but it usually consists of a spirit guide (demon) telling them which one to read for the specific person. Quite literally, demons guide this entire process. These are divination tools that channel demons. Leviticus 19:31 (NKJV) states, "Give no regard to mediums and familiar spirits; do not seek after them, to be defiled by them: I am the LORD your God." God repeatedly reminded His people that He was the Lord God. To fall sway or give credence to mediums and familiar spirits is an attempt to displace God as Lord.

Galatians 5:19–21 outlines what the works of the flesh look like. Sorcery is included in the list, and Paul says, "Those who practice such things will not inherit the kingdom of God" (v. 21). When you let someone use any of these cards on you, you're opening a door for demons. You don't need a card to tell you your future. You need to go to God, and He will unveil it. The Bible says God orders the steps of the righteous. He has it all planned out. Stop stressing. Tarot cards open the door for demons not only in you but also in your home.

Ouija boards

I want you to look at the Wikipedia definition of Ouija and decide whether you think this is something that should be in the home of a Christian:

> The Ouija, also known as a spirit board, talking board, or witch board, is a flat board marked with the letters of the Latin alphabet, the numbers 0–9, the words "yes," "no," and occasionally "hello" and "goodbye," along with various symbols and graphics. It uses a planchette (a small heart-shaped piece of wood or plastic) as a movable indicator to spell out messages during a séance. Participants place their fingers on the planchette, which is moved about the board to spell words. The name 'Ouija' is a trademark of Hasbro but is often used generically to refer to any talking board. Spiritualists in the United States believed that the dead could contact the living, and they reportedly used a talking board very similar to a modern Ouija board at their camps in the U.S. state of

Ohio in 1886 to ostensibly enable faster communication with spirits.[6]

Ouija boards have one purpose, and that is to contact the dead. Christians understand that once you die, you go to heaven or hell; there is no such thing as wandering the earth once you die. People who attempt to talk to their dead relatives or friends via this board are actually engaging with familiar spirits (demons) pretending to be their family or friends.

Isaiah 8:19 (NIV) says, "When someone tells you to consult mediums and spiritists, who whisper and mutter, should not a people inquire of their God? Why consult the dead on behalf of the living?" The Bible warns us about communicating with the dead; this is strictly forbidden. In fact, the first rule of the Ouija board is never to mention God, or you will upset the spirits. That should tell us everything we need to know as Christians! Stay away from this board. It is not a game or a joke. It is an open invitation to demonic spirits into your home and life.

Dream catchers

A few years back my wife and I stayed at an Airbnb cabin in the snow with our kids. The room we slept in had very high ceilings, and at the top was a dream catcher above our bed. I knew these things were demonic, but I had no ladder or way of reaching it, so I left it alone. Also, this wasn't my house, so I didn't really want to get in trouble for moving things around. That night, I had the worst sleep of my life: nightmares, waking up in a cold sweat, hearing things—it was just terrible. The next day, it dawned on me—the dream catcher! I ended up building a long rod with a bunch of old metal hangers and taking it down. Guess what happened? I slept like a baby for the next four nights! When I started to look into the origin of dream catchers, it all began to make sense. These things are demonic.

An excerpt from an article on Harpo's website says about dream catchers and their purpose, "The canvas is responsible for catching bad dreams and evil spirits during the night, and getting rid of them when the day comes. Feathers, on the other hand, allow beautiful dreams to reach the sleeper."[7]

Tiny Rituals says, "Dream catchers do the work of trapping bad energy."[8] As you can see, much of the talk around dream catchers is from New Age and witchcraft. The irony of dream catchers is that they do not ward off evil spirits but instead invite them. Mark and avoid dream catchers at all costs.

Religious statues

This includes statues of Mary, Buddha, Hindu gods, Greek or Roman gods, or any other godlike figures or figurines. The second of the Ten Commandments states that we should not make idols and worship or serve them. This commandment first appears in Exodus 20:4–6 (NASB):

> You shall not make for yourself an idol, or any likeness of what is in heaven above or on the earth beneath or in the water under the earth. You shall not worship them or serve them; for I, the LORD your God, am a jealous God, visiting the iniquity of the fathers on the children, on the third and the fourth generations of those who hate Me, but showing lovingkindness to thousands, to those who love Me and keep My commandments.

The commandment also appears in Deuteronomy 4:15–19 and 23–25, 5:7–9, and 27:15. The common message of these passages is that we are prohibited from making an idol of anything. Deuteronomy 4:23–25 connects the making of an idol to the purpose of worshipping it.

The Hebrew term for *idol, pesel,* is translated as "graven image" or simply "image."[9] It can be crafted from various materials such as clay, wood, stone, silver, gold, or metal. Essentially, an idol or image can be fashioned from anything. The primary concern lies in the intention behind the creation of the idol. Leviticus 19:4 and 26:1 shed light on the correlation between crafting idols and the act of worshipping them. This was a major issue in Bible times, not only the creation and ownership of an idol but the people actually worshipping it. Leviticus 19:4 (NASB) says, "Do not turn to idols or make for yourselves molten gods; I am the LORD your God." Leviticus 26:1 (NASB) says, "You shall not make for yourselves idols, nor shall you set up for yourselves an image or a sacred pillar, nor shall you place a figured stone in your land to bow down to it; for I am the LORD your God." Our God is jealous and will not tolerate idol worship.

Many Catholics worldwide have statues of Mary in their homes. It's essential for us to recognize that the reverence given to Mary equates to worshipping her. According to the *Merriam-Webster* dictionary, *venerate* involves offering "reverential respect," while *worship* entails showing reverence to a divine being.[10] Notably, both definitions emphasize reverence. Despite the Roman Catholic Church's claim that they don't extend the same reverence to Mary as they do to God, they label it veneration to avoid the notion of worship. Worship can be defined as ascribing worth to something or, more elaborately, as demonstrating respect, love, reverence, or adoration. Based on these definitions, there's no distinct disparity between veneration and worship.

When Roman Catholics pray to Mary, they treat her as though she were God. Throughout the Bible prayer is exclusively directed to God Himself, with the exception of Isaiah 45:20, which condemns those who pray to idols. This underscores that prayer should be offered solely to God, not to Mary. Unbeknownst to many Roman Catholics, they inadvertently elevate Mary to the status of a deity, contravening the second commandment.

Burning sage/incense

In the realm of the occult and New Age, burning sage ("smudging") or incense is used to ward off evil spirits. Once again, the irony is that this practice actually attracts them. Those who burn sage/incense are giving demons an open invitation. An article from Healthline says this about sage: "Burning sage has long been used to connect to the spiritual realm or enhance intuition. For healers and laypeople in traditional cultures, burning sage is used to achieve a healing state—or to solve or reflect upon spiritual dilemmas. Burning sage may also be used as a ritual tool to rid yourself or your space of negativity."[11]

Katie Brindle, a Chinese medicine practitioner with over twenty years of clinical experience, sums it up by saying, "Burning sage, also known as cleansing or smudging, is a centuries-old ancient ritual used by people across many cultures as a way to cleanse, purify and heal both living and sacred spaces. It is said to dispel negativity, promote healing, enhance energies, and instill wisdom by connecting to higher realms."[12]

As you can see from these secular articles, this is a spiritual practice that occultists use to so-call "clean energy." We as Christians know this is not a biblical principle, and the Bible tells us to steer clear of divination and occult practices. You may love your sage and your incense, but you must choose today to get rid of anything God is asking you to get rid of so you can walk free in the calling He has for you.

This list is by no means exhaustive; many other things could possibly open up your home to demonic spirits. I urge you to ask the Holy Spirit if there is anything in your home He wants you to get rid of. Here are three quick and simple steps you can do today to rid your house of demons.

1. Destroy every item that gives demons legal rights.

You read that right: Destroy whatever is giving these demons a legal right to be in your home. The ones I listed are a good place to start, but I want you to ask the Holy Spirit if there is anything in your house giving a demon a legal right to be there. If there is, do what they did in the Book of Acts and burn it! You may be tempted to sell it if the item is of value, but I like to say we don't sell our idols; we burn them. Maybe it's a collection of horror movies; maybe it's pouring alcohol down the drain; maybe it's pornographic material; maybe it's a Ouija board; maybe it's an African death mask; maybe it's an evil-eye pendant or a beaded Santeria bracelet. Whatever it is, get rid of it today. Do not let time pass. It's likely you will talk yourself out of getting rid of it.

> Dedicate your house to God and ask the Holy Spirit to permeate it. Tell Him, "This house is Yours. You rule over this place!"

2. Pray out loud in every room, commanding the demons to leave.

For this I want you to get vocal and take authority over every demon in your home. You can pray something like this: "I take authority over every unclean spirit in this house; I command you to leave now in the name of Jesus and never return. You have no legal right or authority here. *Go now!* You have been defeated, and the blood of Jesus is against you; go now in Jesus' name!" Don't be shy about this. The demons haven't been shy about harassing you, so don't be shy about harassing them.

3. Dedicate your house to the Lord, and invite the Holy Spirit in.

This is the most important step: Have a prayer meeting in your house where you dedicate it to God and ask the Holy Spirit to permeate your physical house. Pray this prayer: "Holy Spirit, I invite You into my home; God, I dedicate my house to Your honor and

Your glory. Lord, I am asking You to use my home as a resting place for Your presence; God, do whatever You want to do here. This house is yours. This place will be a headquarters for the Holy Spirit. Lord, I pray if there is anything unclean here, You would drive it out. I pray that You would keep this house clean and pure by Your blood. All the people in this house are dedicated to You and belong to You. Satan, you have no legal authority here. This house has already been claimed. Lord, You rule over this place. In Jesus' name, amen!"

Now that you can identify how demons have gotten in and you have driven them out, you must keep them out! Make sure every spiritual door stays closed and every entrance is locked. You will be shocked at how the atmosphere in your house changes when you get rid of all the items I listed. To God be the glory!

Chapter 7
SEVEN STEPS TO CASTING OUT DEMONS

I F YOU'VE EVER attended Bible college or seminary, you already know there's a class for just about everything—how to write a sermon, how to study and interpret a biblical text, how to communicate effectively using stories and illustrations, how to lead worship, how to write a song, how to start small groups, how to pray, and the list goes on. But you will be hard-pressed to find anything on how to cast out demons practically.

One of the main things Jesus did when He was on the earth was something He commissioned every disciple to do and something we see the early church doing in the Book of Acts. Yet in today's Christian landscape it's not being taught or talked about. This chapter is why I decided to write this book: to give people brand-new to deliverance ministry or those who have done it for years simple and practical steps to casting out demons. Many people are hesitant to pray for someone who is demonized simply because they don't know what to do or where to start.

This chapter will answer those questions and help you begin the journey of deliverance ministry.

I did my best to keep these seven steps as simple as possible while equipping you with everything you need to conduct a deliverance. Remember, deliverance sessions are often dynamic, meaning no two are ever the same, and things change fast. The Holy Spirit is your guide, empowering you to adapt and respond in the moment. Do not be dogmatic or ritualistic about the steps I'm going to give you, as these just provide a baseline to get you started. Not every step is always required for someone to receive complete freedom. At the end of the day it is not these methods or steps that set people free but the power of the Holy Spirit and the authority of Christ. God is the One doing the work; God is the One doing the heavy lifting. We are privileged enough to play a part in this entire process.

If we put too much of our focus on methods and not enough on the Holy Spirit, we will miss what God is trying to do. With that being said, in every deliverance I do, I usually go through all seven of the steps outlined, but there are times when the Holy Spirit does or says something different. When that happens, I go off the script and follow His lead. The following steps are designed for one-on-one ministry but also work when praying at the altar for people; you just may not have the time to be as thorough. If you're confused by the difference, let me explain.

DELIVERANCE ENVIRONMENTS— AND A FEW GROUND RULES

I would place deliverance ministry into two categories: altar deliverance and personal deliverance. At the altar it is more of a power encounter and less strategic than personal deliverance. With altar deliverance let's say you're on the altar prayer team and the pastor calls up anyone who needs deliverance prayer.

The music is playing in the background, and maybe fifteen to twenty minutes are allocated to prayer. Someone comes up, and as you pray, they begin to manifest; at this point it's just you and them. You don't have a team with you, you don't have forty-five minutes to talk to them prior, and you don't have time to take them through all the steps I'm going to break down in this chapter—it's just a few minutes of deliverance prayer. In that case I would begin to command the demons out in Jesus' name and not worry so much about doing all the steps in order.

I believe when you're at the altar in the presence of God, there is grace to drive out demons quickly. I see these deliverances as more of driving the demon out using brute force instead of strategy. The issue with having such a short amount of time is that it's likely not every demon will leave. Usually, with altar deliverance, I tell people, "You have received some freedom, but you will probably need a follow-up with the prayer team one-on-one to ensure nothing is left." Some people get completely free at the altar in five or ten minutes, but it's just not as likely or common. I highly recommend people go for personal deliverance, as there is usually more time and ability to be thorough and ensure every demon is gone.

I would define *personal deliverance* as meeting at a neutral location, such as your house, the home of the person being delivered, a prayer room at a church, or somewhere similar. I recommend having two or three people help you in this process and allocating at least two hours for a session. Sometimes it's good to say we are setting aside two hours no matter what, and if more prayer needs to happen, we can schedule something else at a later date.

Let's say you have three people total. I recommend that one person lead the prayer. (Never have two people trying to lead; it only breeds confusion.) The second person can support and pray lightly under their breath and ask the Holy Spirit for guidance and words of knowledge. The third person can take notes of any demons manifesting or anything that might be relevant later on in the deliverance. The reason it's important to take notes is that toward the end of the deliverance, when we feel as if everything has left, we will once more call out each demon by name to make sure they are not still hiding.

As a male I will never, under any circumstance, pray for a woman alone; I always have other women with me helping to pray, just to be safe and avoid any appearance of evil. If I were a female, I would recommend never meeting up alone with a male to pray, as you can put yourself in a dangerous position. I highly recommend having at least one other person, preferably the sex of the person you're praying for, supporting you during the personal deliverance. Let me also recommend that when doing personal deliverance, you not have a large group, as it becomes too much of a show. I usually never have more than three others helping in a personal deliverance.

Also, be sure the person is wearing comfortable clothing that is not revealing. Things can get violent during deliverance, and oftentimes the person will start thrashing around, and you do not want them to reveal any private areas. Lastly, do not have anyone in the room who is lacking in faith or not ready to be a part of deliverance. Having someone with unbelief will hinder the deliverance, and when people ask me if their family member can sit in, I usually tell them no. For example, when doing deliverance on someone's husband, I recommend the wife not be present, as it could hinder the deliverance and hinder what information is shared.

To recap, altar deliverance is dynamic, is often fast-paced, and takes place in the moment. A personal deliverance is planned and affords the opportunity to take your time and be thorough without trying to rush because a service is ending. Now that you understand deliverance environments better, let me take you through all seven steps of casting out a demon.

Step 1: Make sure the person is a believer and wants to be free.

We have already covered in a previous chapter why I believe Christians can have demons, but let me be clear on something. I *only* pray deliverance over believers or those who want to become believers. The reason is very simple: If the person does not get filled with something to fill the void the demon left, the demons will come back worse. I have seen this happen over and over: Someone who is not a believer gets some deliverance, then goes right back to their sin, and the demons come back seven times worse.

Matthew 12:43–45 (NKJV) says,

> When an unclean spirit goes out of a man, he goes through dry places, seeking rest, and finds none. Then he says, "I will return to my house from which I came." And when he comes, he finds it empty, swept, and put in order. Then he goes and takes with him seven other spirits more wicked than himself, and they enter and dwell there, and the last state of that man is worse than the first. So shall it also be with this wicked generation.

Did you catch that? Because the house remains empty after the demons leave, the demons come back even worse, so why would we do deliverance on an unbeliever if the demons are going to come back worse? Also, it is extremely difficult to cast demons out of someone if the demons have a legal right to stay. In the case of unbelievers they have plenty of legal rights to remain. There is an exception I would make to this rule. Suppose someone who is not a believer wants freedom and chooses to follow Jesus and serve Him. I would then be willing to pray deliverance over them, but before doing so, I would lead them in a prayer of fully surrendering their life to Christ.

Another essential component is that the person wants to be free, and I mean desperate. Just as God recognizes free will, so do demons. If the person genuinely does not want to be free, the demons will recognize that and refuse to leave. My general rule of thumb is you have to want to be set free more than I want you to be set free. I have been in situations where I am praying for deliverance over someone, and I can tell they are bored and disinterested. I will immediately stop the deliverance and let them know that if I want this more than they do, I cannot continue.

> I only pray deliverance over believers or those who want to become believers. The reason is simple: If the person does not get filled with something to fill the void the demon left, the demons will come back worse.

It's very important that the person receiving deliverance participates in their deliverance and helps out in any way possible; this might mean they are telling you what the demons are saying to them or simply staying engaged throughout the entire process. Do not feel bad if you realize someone doesn't want freedom, and tell them you can no longer help them. Too many people want freedom to waste your time on those who do not.

Lastly, never force deliverance on someone; it's almost always ineffective. Mothers come up to me with their teenagers all the time, asking me to pray for deliverance, but when I ask the teenagers if they want to be free, they usually say no. In that case I will not waste my time trying to force them to be delivered. Like salvation, deliverance is a choice someone must make.

Step 2: Lead them through prayers of renouncing, dealing with unforgiveness, and verbally commanding the demons to leave.

Now that you know they want freedom and are believers, this is where the deliverance begins. I can't overstate how important this step is before even confronting the demons. You will now lead the person through the process of renouncing. To renounce simply means to deny something; the person is basically saying, "I sever attachment to this [particular thing], and I no longer want it in my life." Remember, the demons are there because they were invited somehow. This is saying, *"I do not want you in my life any longer."*

When they renounce the demon, they are breaking its legal right to be there. I usually start with the main three to five things they are dealing with and make them verbally say, "I renounce lust, I renounce hate, I renounce witchcraft, I renounce addiction, I renounce perversion," and so forth. If there's something they feel they can't say verbally, there is probably a demon there preventing them, so encourage them to push through, and take note of that for when it's time to confront the demons.

Second Timothy 2:19 says, "But God's truth stands firm like a foundation stone with this inscription: 'The Lord knows those who are his,' and 'All who belong to the Lord must turn away from evil.'" This is not speaking specifically of renouncing before a deliverance, but renouncing is a biblical principle and very powerful. Titus 2:12 (ESV) says, "Training us to *renounce* ungodliness and worldly passions, and to live self-controlled, upright, and godly lives in the present age" (emphasis added). The Holy Spirit may also give you a word of knowledge about something for the person to renounce; even if it sounds crazy or far-fetched, do it anyway. I have come to find it is better to renounce more than less.

Dealing with unforgiveness is the next thing you want to do and should not be rushed. Demons have the ability to root themselves into unforgiveness and use it as a legal right to stay, so make sure the person verbally forgives anyone they harbor unforgiveness toward. I often say unforgiveness is like drinking poison and expecting the other person to die. It only hurts and harms you. In 2 Corinthians 2:10 (KJV) Paul says, "To whom ye forgive any thing, I forgive also: for if I forgave any thing, to whom I forgave it, for your sakes forgave I it in the person of Christ; lest Satan should get an advantage of us: for we are not ignorant of his devices." Look at how Paul connects forgiving someone with the fact that if you do forgive, Satan will not have an advantage over you. So if you don't forgive, you give Satan an advantageous position in your life.

The last part of step 2 is having the person verbally tell the demons they do not want them there. I would lead them through a prayer like this: "I command every demon to leave me now. I do not want you any longer, I am not your home, and you must go now in Jesus' name. I am a child of God and no longer live in the kingdom of darkness. Christ is my Master, and I am a temple of the Holy Spirit. Every unclean spirit must leave me *now*, in Jesus' name." Of course, they don't need to say this word for word, but something like this is powerful in letting the demons know they no longer want them in their life.

Step 3: Confront the demon.

At this point the person may already show signs of a demon manifesting. Usually, during the renouncing portion, the demons have already been stirred up and are beginning to show themselves. The key to deliverance is that the demons must be

110

confronted; you need to talk to them boldly and not back down. Let the person know beforehand, "Hey, I may sound a bit aggressive or harsh, but I'm not talking to you like that; I am talking to the demons. Remember, these things are evil, vile personalities that have no mercy on their victims. This is not the time to confront them nicely."

Next, start calling out the demons you know are likely there; for example, if someone tells you they are struggling with lust, you can begin by saying, "I command the spirit of lust to go now in Jesus' name. Spirit of lust, I know you're there. It's time to come up and out and go into the abyss." You can ask the person receiving deliverance if they feel any reaction to you calling out specific demons or if they are hearing anything in their mind. It's likely the demons will be chattering by now and the person will hear them talking and panicking.

> Unforgiveness is like drinking poison and expecting the other person to die. It only hurts and harms you.

If the demons aren't manifesting, you can do a few things. For clarity, the word *manifest* means to bring something to the light; by manifesting, I mean the demons have made themselves known by talking through the person and so forth. You can plead the blood of Jesus against them; they hate that. You can have the person look you in the eye; for whatever reason, demons hate looking Spirit-filled believers in the eye, and often this causes the demon to manifest. You can put on some worship music, begin to worship, and ask God's presence to fill the room; remember, the very presence of Jesus caused demons to manifest in Scripture. You can pray the fire of God against the demon. You can anoint the person with anointing oil. You can do various things to make the demon surface. The Holy Spirit will lead and guide you as to what step to take.

If someone is manifesting and a demon is talking out of them, and you want the demon to stop, you can call the person back by name and say something like, "I command Ashley to come back. I no longer want to talk to you, spirit." Usually this will stop the demon from manifesting, and the person will gain full control of themselves again. If you're wondering if it's possible to receive deliverance without manifesting a demon, the answer is absolutely. In Luke 13 the woman with the spirit of infirmity did not manifest, to our knowledge, but did get set free. Our goal is not for a demon to manifest; our goal is for the person to get free. Now that the demon is manifesting and you have confronted it, it's time for step 4.

Step 4: Bind the demon in Jesus' name, and command it to go into the abyss.

Matthew 16:19 (NKJV) says, "And I will give you the keys of the kingdom of heaven, and whatever you bind on earth will be bound in heaven, and whatever you loose on earth will be loosed in heaven." This is where the principle of binding and loosing comes into play. When the Scripture mentions "heaven," it refers to the spiritual realm. The term *bind* means to arrest or tie something up. In the spiritual realm we have the power to bind or arrest demonic spirits that are not authorized to be there. Now that the demon is bound, where do we send it?

The Bible does not give a lot of information on where we should send the demon, so this can be subjective, but personally, I command them to go into the abyss, or the pit (they are the same thing). The reason is that in Luke 8:31 the demons begged Jesus not to send them back into the deep, or the abyss. So if the demons do not want to go there, that seems like a good place to send them.

Romans 10:7 says the abyss is the place of the dead, Revelation 17 says the Antichrist will rise out of the abyss, and Revelation 20 says the abyss is where Satan will be bound for a thousand years before getting released again. In Revelation 9 the abyss is described as an area under the earth with some shaft where smoke comes out like a furnace. My thoughts are that the abyss is where demons wait until judgment. To me the abyss, or pit, is a safe place to send them. Some people send them to the feet of Jesus, which doesn't make sense to me, as Jesus is seated at the right hand of the Father. Why would we send demons to heaven? In one instance Jesus did allow demons to enter pigs, but this was not normative, so I would not make a practice out of it.

I have noticed that when demons leave, they often leave through the mouth; this might be through a loud scream, a long yawn, or even coughing. Gagging and feeling as if you want to vomit are normal in a deliverance, as this is simply the demon making its way up through the esophagus, causing you to gag. There will sometimes be signs of the demon leaving. For example, Mark 9:26 says, "Then the spirit screamed and threw the boy into another violent convulsion and left him. The boy appeared to be dead. A murmur ran through the crowd as people said, 'He's dead.'" This is common when a demon leaves. At times you will know a demon leaves because the person goes limp or seems lifeless. Demonic spirits usually leave through a loud scream, according to Acts 8:7: "For unclean spirits, crying with a loud voice, came out of many who were possessed [demonized]: and many who were paralyzed and lame were healed."

There is an unlimited number of ways a demon might leave someone. I am mentioning only the most common. Just because these do not happen during the deliverance does not mean the demon hasn't left.

Step 5: If the demon doesn't leave, find out why.

I'm not going to go into great detail on this, as I have dedicated an entire chapter to dealing with stubborn demons, but I will say there is always a reason a demon is disobedient. This could be that they still have a legal right to be there, in which case you may need to go back and have the person renounce something or deal with unforgiveness again. I have, at times, been in deliverance for several hours, only to find out the demon is not leaving because the person still has unforgiveness toward someone. To find out why they are not leaving, you can simply say, "I command you to tell me why you won't leave. What legal right do you have to be here?" The demon may then verbally speak out of the person and tell you why, or the person might hear the reason in their mind. Interacting with the person and asking them what they hear is important.

During this portion of the deliverance it's easy to get frustrated. Do your best to stay patient and calm, and if you need to, take a five-to-ten-minute break, drink some water, and regroup. I would also inquire of the others helping you pray and ask their thoughts; they may have a word of knowledge or insight as to why the demons are not leaving or why the deliverance is stalling out. I've had many experiences where I felt stuck and didn't know what to do next. In one instance I asked one of my ministry partners for help, and they gave a word of knowledge that kept the deliverance going. Refer to my chapter dealing with stubborn demons for an in-depth guide on what to do when demons don't listen.

Step 6: Go back and make sure everything is gone.

Demons are very good at hiding, and at this point of the deliverance you may feel as if you're done and the person is completely free. I highly advise going back through to make sure nothing is left. You should have had someone taking notes and keeping track of what demons manifested and what demons revealed themselves. I would now say something like, "I command the spirit of lust to reveal itself; I command the spirit of anger to reveal itself; I command any hiding demon to manifest itself now in Jesus' name." What you're trying to do is make sure the demons you thought left didn't go back into hiding. Sometimes demons will fool you into thinking they left when really they are just hiding.

When commanding the demons to leave again, look at body language; if the person starts twitching or reacting in a weird way, it might be a sign the demon is still hiding. Sometimes I will look the person in the eyes and be able to see in the spirit realm that the demon is still there, or it may just begin to manifest again. You're probably tired at this point and want to be done, but do your best to finish the job. It is much easier to finish a deliverance you have already started than to bring the person back another day and try to finish it. I will also ask the Holy Spirit for a word of knowledge and to confirm that everything is gone. If I feel peace in my spirit, I will go to the last step; if not, I will continue to apply pressure on the demons that might be hiding.

Step 7: Pray for the Holy Spirit to fill them.

Although this is last, it is certainly not the least! Now that the demons are gone, as Jesus says in Matthew 12, the house is empty. It needs to be filled—that is, filled with the Holy Spirit! I teach people a simple four-step process to help them receive the baptism of the Holy Spirit.

1. Repent. Peter reveals this to us in Acts 2:38: We must repent. There is no way to get around it. To repent is to completely turn away from our rebellion and sinfulness to say, Lord, change how I think; I am wrong. You are right, and I want You to change me. Repentance is not a one-time thing. It's a lifestyle. Acts 17:30 (ESV) says, "The times of ignorance God overlooked, but now he commands all people everywhere to repent." Repentance is essential to receiving the baptism of the Holy Spirit.

2. Ask God for it. Luke 11:11–13 (NKJV) says,

> If a son asks for bread from any father among you, will he give him a stone? Or if he asks for a fish, will he give him a serpent instead of a fish? Or if he asks for an egg, will he offer him a scorpion? If you then, being evil, know how to give good gifts to your children, how much more will your heavenly Father give the Holy Spirit to those who ask Him!

Some say if God wants me to have it, He will give it to me. That is not scriptural; you need to ask!

3. Be thirsty. John 7:37–39 (NIV) says,

> On the last and greatest day of the festival, Jesus stood and said in a loud voice, "Let anyone who is thirsty come to me and drink. Whoever believes in me, as Scripture has said, rivers of living water will flow from within them." By this, he meant the Spirit, whom those who believed in him were later to receive. Up to that time, the Spirit had not been given since Jesus had not yet been glorified.

We must be thirsty. God does not force His blessings on those who don't feel they need them. Many people never receive the fullness of the Spirit because they are not really thirsty. If you think you already have all you need, why should God bother you with more? To be thirsty is essential. It means you recognize you need more than you already have. Thirst is one of the strongest desires in the human body. When people are really thirsty, they do not care about eating or satisfying other needs. All they want is something to drink. Jesus says this has to be all you want.

4. You must drink! Then Jesus said you must "drink" (John 7:37). This is so simple that some people don't discuss it. In a natural sense, to drink is to receive something within you by a decision of your will and a physical act. A similar process is required for receiving the Holy Spirit. Being passive means saying, "Well, if God wants to do it, let Him do it!" That response is not drinking. To drink is to receive within you actively.

To summarize:

1. Make sure the person is a believer and wants to be free.

2. After that, lead them through renunciation prayers and dealing with unforgiveness.

3. Confront the demon in Jesus' name.

4. Bind the demon in Jesus' name, and command it to go to the abyss.

5. If the demon doesn't leave, find out why.

6. Once the demon has left, go back through and check to make sure nothing remains.

7. Finally, you can pray for the person to be filled with the Holy Spirit so their house (body) does not remain empty.

What happens if you encounter stubborn demons that refuse to leave? That's where we're going next. Read on.

Chapter 8

DEALING WITH STUBBORN DEMONS

ONE OF THE longest deliverances I've ever done lasted almost seven hours. From the outside the woman needing deliverance seemed completely normal. She was successful in her field, was well put together, and did not look like someone you would think had an uncountable number of demons. I had a flight home to catch in the afternoon, but considering we started her deliverance early in the morning, I didn't think I would miss my flight.

She told us what she was going through, and I thought, "Oh, this won't be longer than maybe thirty minutes," as her symptoms were not very severe. Boy, was I wrong. As we began to pray for her from the start of the deliverance, the manifestations were severe. She was thrashing, screaming, hissing at us, and slithering on the ground like a snake. This continued for hours. What we did not know was that her family from Puerto Rico was heavily involved in witchcraft for many generations, and the demons we were dealing with had been in the family for many years.

It got so bad that for the first time in over a decade of doing deliverance I felt afraid for a moment. She was on all fours upside down, and her head was spinning backward in a way that should be physically impossible. I had a cold chill down my back for almost an hour and noticed that some of the prayer team, including the pastor's wife, was getting scared. We gave the woman a bathroom break, and I told the prayer team not to show any signs of fear, as the demons would play on that.

We were writing down the names of the demons manifesting, and after fifty we stopped keeping track. To say these demons were stubborn would be an understatement. At the four-hour mark, we had been wrestling with one specific ancient demon for forty-five minutes, and I thought there had to be a way to get this stubborn demon out.

I recalled a deliverance method exorcist Bob Larson uses. He has been doing deliverance for over forty years and has documented more than fifty thousand deliverances. He makes the demon repeat after him and declare its demise. I usually do not use that method, but I thought, "What do we have to lose? We've been at this for four hours, and my flight leaves in a few hours. We have to finish this and get this lady free." Sure enough, I made the demon repeat after me and declare its defeat, and all the demons began to leave one after another. We ended up finishing the deliverance minutes before I had to head to the airport, and I realized how truly stubborn demons can be. I also realized there are things we can do to be more efficient and effective when dealing with stubborn demons. In my case it was changing my method.

Without a doubt one of the most frustrating and discouraging things you will encounter when starting to do deliverance is dealing with stubborn demons. Those who don't practice deliverance might think that every demon obeys at the first command in Jesus' name. But even in the case of the demonized man at the tombs in Mark 5, Jesus had already commanded the demon out of the man. The demon did not listen, and then Jesus asked its name. I am not quite sure how, but this demon was able to withstand even the Son of God for a few minutes.

It is no shock, though, that demons are stubborn, as their leader, Satan, is also stubborn. He rebelled against God in heaven and was cast down, and when he had the opportunity to deceive humanity in the garden, he did. His goal was to get Adam and Eve to disobey God and not listen to God's command, which is the epitome of being stubborn. Sadly, in the case of Adam and Eve he succeeded.

Isaiah 14:12–15 shows just how stubborn Satan is in describing his fall from heaven.

> How you are fallen from heaven, O shining star, son of the morning! You have been thrown down to the earth, you who destroyed the nations of the world. For you said to yourself, "I will ascend to heaven and set my throne above God's stars. I will preside on the mountain of the gods far away in the north. I will climb to the highest heavens and be like the Most High." Instead, you will be brought down to the place of the dead, down to its lowest depths.

Here we see Satan's true stubborn nature, to get glory for himself and be like God. Instead, he is cast out of heaven and banished to the earth. This stubborn nature Satan possesses is also an attribute the demons who fell with him possess.

I'll say it again: One of the most discouraging aspects of doing deliverance, especially when starting out, is when demons don't obey you and the deliverance stalls out. Many scratch their heads, wondering what they are doing wrong, as nothing seems to be working. Others quit after their first attempt because they feel that deliverance doesn't work. Let me encourage you: Do not be discouraged. We have all dealt with this. I often still deal with this even after years of experience and doing countless deliverances. Demons have incredible strength to fight and resist those trying to cast them out, and they can remain stubborn for several reasons. Let me discuss a few things you can do to overcome stubborn demons.

1. Remind the demon they are defeated.

Stubborn demons believe they are stronger than you and have more authority and power than you do. When they say, "I don't have to leave; I am stronger than you. You can't cast me out. You are not strong enough; I'm never leaving," this is when I declare Scripture, reminding them they have no power and authority here. Christ is the only One in charge and in authority, and I am coming in His name and authority. Speaking the truth weakens the demon. I highly recommend memorizing some of the following verses so you can quote them quickly in the heat of the battle.

I might say something like, "Your leader has been defeated. Luke 10:18—Jesus said, 'I saw Satan fall from heaven like lightning!' You and your leader have fallen from the place of authority; you have no power here." Trust me, they hate it when you quote this verse! This might sound too simple for you, but we must remember that in Matthew 4 Jesus overcame the devil in the wilderness by quoting Scripture. This is a powerful tool against these stubborn demons. As you quote the Word, they often begin to scream in agony, begging you to stop.

I will then remind the demons that I have authority over them. They do not have it over me or their victim. I will quote the next verse, "Luke 10:19—Behold, I have given you authority to tread on serpents and scorpions, and over all the power of the enemy, and nothing shall hurt you." I will remind them that I have authority to tread on them, and I have been given authority from Jesus Christ of Nazareth over all the power of the enemy. I will also remind them of their future torment in the lake of fire and quote Revelation 20:10: "Then the devil, who had deceived them, was thrown into the fiery lake of burning sulfur, joining the beast and the false prophet. There they will be tormented day and night forever and ever." There are many verses you can quote to weaken stubborn demons. These are just a few good ones to start with. Ultimately, you're speaking truth where they are speaking lies and overcoming them with the Word of God.

2. Bind the strongman.

If you're dealing with a demon that will not listen to you or is continually disobedient to the command to leave, you can ask to speak to the strongman, or the chief demon in the person. I have found that inside anyone who is demonized, there is always one demon in charge that governs all the other lower-ranking demons. What usually happens is the strongest demon will send out the lower-ranking demons to talk and distract you as long as he

> Stubborn demons believe they are stronger and have more power than you do. When they say, "I don't have to leave," remind them that Christ is the only One in charge and in authority.

can. He will usually try to be the last one to leave. Instead of wasting time on low-ranking, pesky demons, I want to speak to the strongman, or the chief demon.

We learn about the strongman right after the Pharisees accuse

Jesus of being the prince of demons because He was casting out demons. In Matthew 12:28 Jesus responds to their allegations and says, "But if I am casting out demons by the Spirit of God, then the Kingdom of God has arrived among you. For who is powerful enough to enter the house of a strong man and plunder his goods? Only someone even stronger—someone who could tie him up and then plunder his house."

To bind the strongman, we first need to identify who the strongman of the house is. By this point of the book I have already explained on multiple occasions that Jesus said demons call us their home (Matt. 12:43). Once again, we see the idea of houses. Once you identify who the strongman is, the next thing you can do is bind him. Matthew 16:19 (BLB) says, "I will give you the keys of the kingdom of the heavens, and whatever you might bind on the earth shall have been bound in the heavens, and whatever you might loose on the earth shall have been loosed in the heavens." This is where we get the principle of binding and loosing.

The word *bind* means to arrest or tie something up. We have power in the Spirit to tie up or arrest demonic spirits that are not authorized to be there. Once it is bound, you can now cast it out and loose the person from this demonic spirit. Remember, in Luke 13 Jesus correlates women being bound by Satan to the Pharisees untying their donkey. Jesus tells them in so many words, "You untie your donkey and loose it on the Sabbath, but you're mad that I untied and loosed this daughter of Abraham who was bound by Satan on the Sabbath?" To plunder the strongman's goods means to take back what he has taken captive. You can now take back your joy, take back your peace, take back your happiness, take back your health, take back your marriage. Whatever the strongman has held, you can now plunder since he is bound and cast out of the house. You will also notice that the lower-ranking demons in the person will not only leave more easily once the strongman is gone but often will all leave with him. I will often say, "I bind the strongman and command him to leave and take everyone under his command with him at once."

3. Take a break and pray and worship.

OK, if you have been dealing with a stubborn demon for a while, it's likely you're exhausted and the person receiving the deliverance is exhausted as well. I know this seems very practical, but I can't stress enough how helpful it is to take a break and spend some time in prayer and worship. Stubborn demons have a way of taking the wind out of our sails, and there is nothing like going to God for a fresh wind from the Holy Spirit. I have a playlist of a few of my favorite deliverance songs, and I might play one and begin to worship and thank God for what He's doing and what He's done. I will thank Him for what He did on the cross and remind myself this is not about me but about Him. This often will break discouragement right off me and fuel me to continue. After some time in worship and magnifying God, I will spend a few minutes in prayer.

> Stubborn demons have a way of taking the wind out of our sails, and there is nothing like going to God for a fresh wind from the Holy Spirit.

This often consists of me asking the Holy Spirit for a word of knowledge or a battle plan to continue. I will ask the Lord, "What am I missing? What can I do differently? Why is this stalling out, or why is this demon not listening to me? Is there some sin that hasn't been confessed? Is there something the person is hanging on to? Is there a strategy

I need to implement?" I will pray something like, "Lord, open my eyes and show me what only You can see." Sometimes when I do this, I will begin to immediately get from the Holy Spirit the names of the demons hiding and how many there are. I will write them down, and then when I go back to praying for deliverance over the person, I start calling out some of the demons the Holy Spirit revealed to me via a word of knowledge that is there. You will be surprised how powerful a small worship and prayer break can be during a deliverance. Rather than spend another ten minutes screaming at the same demon, take a break and let the Holy Spirit speak to you.

4. Recognize and break soul ties.

Stubborn demons like to hang on and attach themselves to ungodly soul ties in our lives. The basic definition of a soul tie is a linkage in the soul realm between two people. Soul ties link their souls together, which can bring forth both beneficial and negative results. The soul realm is the mind, will, and emotions of the person. Not every soul tie is bad. We see in 1 Samuel 18:1 a healthy soul tie; it says, "As soon as he had finished speaking to Saul, the soul of Jonathan was knit to the soul of David, and Jonathan loved him as his own soul." In this case this was a positive soul tie, but in the case of deliverance and for the sake of what we are talking about, they are usually bad.

After I got saved, the Lord revealed to me several soul ties I had with people I had slept with before marriage, and in a series of dreams He revealed these people. I went through the process of breaking these soul ties so I could walk in complete freedom.

Unhealthy soul ties that are demonic in nature usually develop when having sex with someone outside of marriage. I do not reference *The Message* Bible much, but in the case of this verse, I want you to see how *The Message* Bible describes 1 Corinthians 6:16–20. It says:

There's more to sex than mere skin on skin. Sex is as much spiritual mystery as physical fact. As written in Scripture, "The two become one." Since we want to become spiritually one with the Master, we must not pursue the kind of sex that avoids commitment and intimacy, leaving us more lonely than ever—the kind of sex that can never "become one." There is a sense in which sexual sins are different from all others. In sexual sin we violate the sacredness of our own bodies, these bodies that were made for God-given and God-modeled love, for "becoming one" with another. Or didn't you realize that your body is a sacred place, the place of the Holy Spirit? Don't you see that you can't live however you please, squandering what God paid such a high price for? The physical part of you is not some piece of property belonging to the spiritual part of you. God owns the whole works. So let people see God in and through your body.

This is the essence of how a soul tie gets developed. Notice it says through the act of sex, the two become one. That is a connecting of the souls. Why? Because as it says, sex is as much a spiritual mystery as a physical fact. There is something spiritual about the act of sex; God designed it that way so that when you get married, you can, through the act of sex, become one with your wife. The devil has perverted that, and when people have sex before marriage, they unite in an unholy way and develop ungodly and demonic soul ties. Stubborn demons will hang on to these and use them as a legal right to stay. I didn't want to make an entire chapter about soul ties, but you might be reading this wondering if you have a soul tie or how to identify a soul tie, so here are a few ways to know if one is there.

- You picture them in your mind when you're with another person.

- Even after ending the relationship, you find yourself preoccupied with thoughts of them.

- Despite suffering physical, spiritual, or verbal abuse, you feel too connected to leave.

- You justify their behavior when your friends and family highlight the harm they cause you.

- You start adopting the characteristics of the person you feel deeply connected to.

- You frequently dream and fantasize about them.

- You feel unable to move forward with your life.

Now I want to help you break these. You can do this right in the middle of a deliverance if you identify the reason that the demon is stubborn and hanging on. First, you need to forgive the person your soul is tied to. You will have them say, "I forgive (name). I release him/her from the harm he/she caused me. I let it go." You will then lead them in a prayer like this: "I break the unhealthy soul tie between me and (name). I send back any part of their soul that I have kept, and I take back to myself any part of me that they kept. God, please wash me of this connection and restore my connection with You in this area of my soul." I also recommend counseling them to get rid of anything they received from the person their soul was tied to; this could be a T-shirt, jewelry, a gift, or various other things. The bottom line is if a demon is hanging on to this attachment, it needs to be broken for it to finally leave. I have seen this firsthand time and time again.

5. Ask God to send angels to help.

Years ago I was doing a very intense deliverance on a young man who was a professional MMA fighter who came for deliverance because he had uncontrollable rage and anger issues in his life. I mean, it makes sense that his entire life revolved around fighting and violence. I knew there would probably be a violent manifestation, so I had four other guys help me pray for this man. During the deliverance it got so out of hand we could not hold him down or control him, and he was violently thrashing and trying to hit us.

I prayed this exact prayer: "Lord, please send Your angels to come to hold him down; we need Your help." As the words left my mouth, he went from standing up, resisting, and fighting all of us, to immediately on his back with both hands and arms pinned to the ground. I was shocked and amazed that God had just answered my prayer. The demon began to scream, "Get them off me! Get off me!" I responded, "Get who off you?" None of us were touching him. The demon replied to me, saying, "These angels are holding us down! Get them off! We hate them!" This is the first time I asked for angels to help with a violent, stubborn demon, and my eyes were opened to how powerful they really are.

We do not command the angels; it is God who commands them. Psalm 91:11 says, "For he will command his angels concerning you to guard you in all your ways." Biblically, we should not try to command angels but instead ask the Lord to send His angels to help us during a time of need. Hebrews 1:14 says, "Are they not all ministering spirits sent out to serve for the sake of those who are to inherit salvation?" What an amazing statement! Angels are God's spirits that are sent to serve us! If there are angels assigned to serve us, why would we not ask God for those angels to help? Psalm 103:20 says, "Bless the LORD, O you his angels, you mighty ones who do his word, obeying the voice of his word!" So we see here the angels do His word and obey the voice of His word. In Acts 5:19 we actually see an angel opening prison doors and releasing the apostles from prison. Talk about deliverance! Acts 5:19 says, "But during the night an angel of the Lord opened the prison doors and brought them out."

Daniel 10 is a perfect example of angels involved in spiritual warfare. Daniel is fasting and praying for his nation because they are in bondage when suddenly an angel appears to him, and Daniel 10:12–13 says: "Then he said, 'Don't be afraid, Daniel. Since the first day you began to pray for understanding and to humble yourself before your God, your request has been heard in heaven. I have come in answer to your prayer. But for twenty-one days, the spirit prince of the kingdom of Persia blocked my way. Then Michael, one of the archangels, came to help me, and I left him there with the spirit prince of the kingdom of Persia.'"

So Daniel is praying, and God responds by sending an angel; the angel is blocked by a demonic principality of the kingdom of Persia. Michael comes and helps fight, so this angel is able to deliver this message to Daniel. The point of it all is simple: The moment Daniel began to pray, the angel was dispatched to war on his behalf. If, in the Old Testament, God would respond to Daniel by sending an angel to help fight a demonic spirit, how much more in the New Covenant would He answer our prayers for help?

I know it can feel discouraging when dealing with stubborn demons, but remember what Romans 8:37 says: "No, in all these things, we are more than conquerors through him who loved us." At the end of the day we are on the winning side; the demons are subject to us. In Christ's name we are not subject to them. Do not believe their lies that they have more power than you; do not fall for their tricks to distract and discredit you. Keep your eyes on Jesus throughout the entire deliverance process, use some of these strategies I have given you, and most importantly, *do not give up*! Keep fighting until you see the victory. You will overcome these stubborn demons in Jesus' name.

Chapter 9

HOW TO KEEP DEMONS OUT AFTER DELIVERANCE

P EOPLE OFTEN THINK that once deliverance takes place, nothing more needs to be done. That could not be further from the truth. Often after we go through deliverance, there are steps we need to take to make sure the demons don't return or new demons don't seek entrance. In this chapter I want to outline six practical things you can do after deliverance to ensure demons do not return.

Be aware that it's very normal after someone goes through a deliverance for there to be backlash and even the feeling of not being fully delivered. Demons do everything they can to assault you right after you get completely free. The first one to two weeks are the most important. If we can teach people to resist the enemy during this period, the demons will not usually keep trying to come back.

James 4:7 (NIV) says, "Submit yourselves, then, to God. Resist the devil, and he will flee from you." Notice that before we even resist, we must submit to God! If you don't submit to God after your deliverance, you open yourself up to being re-demonized. Most people quote this verse to resist the devil but fail to realize that before you resist him, you need to submit yourself to God. Sadly, in the Western church we resist God and submit to the devil instead of the other way around.

The word *resist* is a verb that *Merriam-Webster* dictionary defines as "to exert oneself so as to counteract or defeat."[1] This is not simply saying no to the devil when he comes; this is actually counteracting or defeating him. So now you're submitted to God, you're fighting against the enemy's attack, and what is the result? The devil runs! Imagine that! Instead of running from demons that try to attack you, demons are running from you because you fight back against them. When Jesus showed up, the demons would say, "Have you come to torment us?" The very presence of Christ torments demons, and that same presence is alive inside you. If you really understand this, it changes the way you fight against Satan's kingdom.

In Matthew 12 Jesus teaches us an extremely important principle when it comes to demons leaving a person and attempting to reenter. Let's dive into this. I want to show you something you may never have seen before. These letters are red in your Bible, meaning they are the words of Jesus, so we should pay extra attention. Let's look at Matthew 12:43–45, which says:

> When an evil spirit leaves a person, it goes into the desert, seeking rest but finding none. Then it says, "I will return to the person I came from." So it returns and finds its former home empty, swept, and in order. Then the spirit finds seven other spirits more evil than itself, and they all enter the person and live there. And so that person is worse off than before. That will be the experience of this evil generation.

Jesus tells us the first thing an evil spirit does when it leaves a person. Whether this is when it's cast out or it has the ability to leave on its own will is not clear, but we know the demon has just left a person. The very first thing it does is look for somewhere dry to rest. Demons love dry Christians, dry churches, dry pastors, dry preaching, dry prayer lives, and dry spirituality. Pretty much anything that is dry is a good place for a demon to rest. We want to make sure our lives are not suitable places for demons to rest! Demons love dry environments. Psalm 22:3 (KJV) says, "But thou art holy, O thou that inhabitest the praises of Israel." How incredible is it that God inhabits environments of praise while demons dwell in dry places.

Next Jesus tells us that the demon says something to itself: "Then it says, 'I will return to the person I came from'" (Matt. 12:44). Here we see the clear intention of a demon that leaves a person. It wants to return! It wants to reenter the person it left. So we now know our job is to make sure it doesn't have the ability to make a reentrance. Our job, once the demon is gone, is to make sure it can't come back even if it wants to,

> The very presence of Christ torments demons, and that same presence is alive inside you. If you really understand this, it changes the way you fight against Satan's kingdom.

and because of this verse we know it wants to. Jesus then says, "So it returns and finds its former home empty, swept, and in order" (v. 44).

Jesus gives us another insight into the mind of demons. They actually treat humans as "homes." Principally, demons live inside human bodies, making the human bodies their homes. Pause reading for a second, and say this out loud: "Devil, I am not your home; you cannot live inside me. You must leave now in Jesus' name!" I take it personally that a demon thinks I am its home. Sometimes I wonder how comfortable I've made my "house" for demons. Some of us want our demons to leave, but we've made them a comfortable house. We give them a nightly snack of compromise and feed them meals of sin all day long. We need to make our "houses" places of prayer and worship so demons no longer want to live inside us. I think some people can be delivered just by changing the way they live!

I vividly remember praying for a girl in South Carolina, and the demon manifested and spoke out of her, saying, "Tell me to leave!" I was shocked and thought, "Wait a minute; the demon wants to leave her?" I responded, "Why do you want to leave?" The demon said, "I don't want to live here. All she does is fast and pray. I hate living in this house!" I said, "Why haven't you left yet?" The demon then said, "Because nobody has told me to!" I was shocked to learn that not only do some demons not want to live in the house (body) they are in, but sometimes they have to have a believer tell them to leave before they are even able to. Let's make our "houses" uncomfortable for demons to live in.

Empty, Swept, and in Order

There are three specific things the demon finds when it returns: The house is (1) empty, (2) swept, and (3) in order. At first glance this seems a bit confusing because you might say, "Well, what's wrong with a house being swept and in order?" (Remember, "house" here refers to a person's body.) The problem is in the word *empty*. The person is empty! The demons are now gone, but that empty space has not been replaced with anything. This is where we need to be filled with the Holy Spirit so demons cannot make reentrance into our lives. Your life might be swept and look clean from the outside, and it might even be in order, but if it's empty, those demons have a legal right to come right back and with their friends this time!

After every deliverance I pray for the person to be filled with the Holy Spirit. We need to make sure our lives are filled with His power and His fruit. Galatians 5:22–23 (NKJV) says, "But the fruit of the Spirit is love, joy, peace, longsuffering, kindness, goodness, faithfulness, gentleness, self-control. Against such, there is no law."

These attributes fill our lives in such a way that there is no room for demons to fester. Demons actually cultivate the opposite of the fruits of the Spirit. Instead of love they birth hate; instead of joy they cause depression and sadness; instead of peace they induce chaos; instead of long-suffering they want you to quit; instead of kindness they exhibit anger; instead of goodness they bring misery; instead of faithfulness they are inconsistent; instead of gentleness they bring harsh words; instead of self-control they cause us to be out of control. They not only do not keep the laws of God; they actually break them. If we want to keep our house filled, we must cultivate the fruits of the Spirit.

> Demons love dry Christians, dry churches, dry pastors, dry preaching, dry prayer lives, and dry spirituality.

Let's continue with the next thing Jesus says in this parable: "Then the spirit finds seven other spirits more evil than itself, and they all enter the person and live there. And so that person is worse off than before" (Matt. 12:45). So not only does that demon try to come back into the person, but it brings its friends who are "more evil" than itself. Not all demons are equal. Some are more evil than others. Jesus says when this happens, that person is worse off than before! It's possible that someone who goes through deliverance and does not take the aftercare seriously will actually be worse off than before they went through deliverance.

This is one of the reasons I *only* do deliverance on Christians. Why would you deliver someone who is in the world, just for them to go back and reopen the same doors the demons came through in the first place—and then be worse off than before? I have seen this happen over and over again throughout the years, and I finally decided I would not do deliverance on someone who was not ready or was not going to follow Jesus afterward.

Notice what Jesus says next: "That will be the experience of this evil generation" (v. 45). Jesus goes from talking about a specific person being demonized to an entire generation. Could it be we have an entire generation that is empty and void of the Holy Spirit, so in the place where God should be, demons reign? We need to see mass deliverance in this generation like never before. I believe we are on the verge of the greatest deliverance revival America has ever seen. We now understand the goal a demon has when it leaves, and that is to reenter you, so let's look at six practical ways we can keep demons out once they have left.

Six Ways to Keep Demons Out

1. Keep the doors closed.

Do not reopen the doors the demons came through originally. Remember, demons were there in the first place because you opened a door to them. The first way to keep them out might sound like an obvious one, but you would be surprised how often people get delivered and then go right back and reopen the door the demons entered through in the first place. If you know a spirit of lust came through watching pornography, you must do everything in your power not to watch pornography. If you know a demon came in through doing drugs, make sure not to return to those same drugs. If a demon entered you through practicing the New Age, get rid of everything that has to do with the New Age. You get the point.

Demons are looking to reenter, and it's usually through the door they came through the first time. The devil does not have creative power, and I've learned he usually will not bring new addictions and temptations into your life after deliverance but instead will entice you with old ones. We all know what our triggers are; these are things that stir up those ungodly desires in us that cause us to sin. You may need to find new friends, you may need to get off social media, and you may need to stop watching TV past 9 p.m. Whatever you need to do to make sure the doors stay closed, do it!

First Corinthians 10:13 (NIV) says, "No temptation has overtaken you except what is common to mankind. And God is faithful; he will not let you be tempted beyond what you can bear. But when you are tempted, he will also provide a way out so that you can endure it." I love how Paul says God will provide a way out. Here is the key to overcoming temptation: When you're tempted, find the exit! There is *always* a way out; you just have to take it. Paul also says there is no temptation you're facing that other people haven't also dealt with. If others have overcome it, so can you. Oftentimes during temptation we choose to run toward the sin instead of running toward the exit. If a building is on fire, the first thing we would do is find the exit and run to it. So why, when the fires of sin are burning in our lives, do we run toward the fire and not take the exit? It sounds silly to run into the fire, yet we do this every time we go back to our old sin.

Here is a helpful scripture that is part of the Lord's Prayer. You can pray it every day if you're struggling with this: Matthew 6:13 (NIV): "And lead us not into temptation, but deliver us from the evil one." You can pray something as simple as this.

> *Lord, I thank You that today You're not leading me toward temptation, but You're leading me away from temptation. I pray, Lord, that today You would deliver me from the evil one and help me stay pure. Help me in my weakness, and help me in my strength. Holy Spirit, I can't do this without You; I need Your grace and power today to say no to the devil and say yes to You. Lord, today I choose to close the door to sin and compromise, and open the door to You! In Jesus' name, amen.*

I guarantee you that if you start praying simple prayers like this every day, it will be much easier to keep the door closed on the devil and keep demons from reentering your life.

2. Speak God's Word over your life.

I cannot stress this enough; you must learn to speak the Scripture throughout your life. There is nothing more powerful than verbally declaring the promises of God. I have noticed that people who are demonized often speak forth negative confessions. They say things like, "I will always be this way," "Things are never going to change," "My parents were like this, so I will be like this," and the list goes on. Talking like this is a great way to attract demons. When you're speaking death over your life, demons listen to that, and they capitalize on it. Negative confessions attract demons, but confessing the Word of God repels demons. In the same way you put on bug spray to keep pesky insects from landing on you, when you speak the Word of God over your life—like a spiritual bug spray—demons hate being around you. Why would a demon want to be around someone who is always quoting Scripture? Why would a demon want to live in a body that is filled with God's Word? As I said earlier, this is about making yourself an uncomfortable home for demons.

Matthew 11:22–24 (NKJV) says, "For assuredly, I say to you, whoever says to this mountain, 'Be removed and be cast into the sea,' and does not doubt in his heart, but believes that those things he says will be done, he will have whatever he says." This scripture makes it clear that our words have power! Mountains don't move when we talk about them. They move when we talk to them. We need to stop telling everyone about our mountain and start telling it to move. Depression, it's time to move! Anger, it's time to move! Sickness, it's time to move! Demons, it's time to move out! Choose today that you will not be moved by life's mountains, but instead, you will move them. I will not be moved by anxiety, but instead, I will move anxiety!

Jesus says the person who does this will have *whatever* he says. That's a pretty bold statement. If you speak death and destruction, that's what you will have, but if you speak the promises of God, that's what you will have. Your words have incredible power in the spiritual realm. Proverbs 18:21 (NIV) says, "The tongue has the power of life and death, and those who love it will eat its fruit." Some of us have been eating some really bad fruit because we've been saying some really bad things. Try changing the way you talk, and you'll notice a drastic difference in your life.

Speaking God's Word strengthens your faith in His promises. Romans 10:17 (ESV) says, "So faith comes from hearing, and hearing through the word of Christ."

Speaking God's Word helps renew your mind according to His truth. Romans 12:2 (ESV) says, "Do not be conformed to this world, but be transformed by the renewal of your mind, that by testing you may discern what is the will of God, what is good and acceptable and perfect."

Speaking God's Word is a powerful weapon against spiritual attacks. Ephesians 6:17 (ESV) says, "And take the helmet of salvation, and the sword of the Spirit, which is the word of God."

Speaking God's Word provides comfort and encouragement in difficult times. Psalm 119:50 (ESV) says, "This is my comfort in my affliction, that your promise gives me life."

Speaking God's Word fosters a deeper relationship with Him. Joshua 1:8 (ESV) says, "This Book of the Law shall not depart from your mouth, but you shall meditate on it day and night, so that you may be careful to do according to all that is written in it. For then you will make your way prosperous, and then you will have good success."

3. Stay in the Scripture.

At first glance this might seem repetitive, like, "Isaiah, your last point was to speak God's Word over your life." There is no such thing as too much of God's Word; it really is our source of life. But we need to stay in the Scripture, not just get in the Scripture. It's one thing to read the Bible every once in a while, or maybe the first few weeks of the new year, and it's a completely different thing to be in the Scripture daily. I am telling you that if you don't develop a daily relationship with the Bible, you will struggle to stay free from demonization. Demons prey on Christians who don't know the Bible.

When the devil tempted Jesus in the wilderness (Matthew 4), Jesus withstood Him by quoting Scripture. Jesus would say, "It is written," and then quote a Bible verse. How could we truly fight against the enemy and stay free if we don't even know what is written? To respond to a demon with "It is written," you have to actually know what is written. Sadly, many in the church rely on Google to tell them what the Bible says instead of actually opening the Bible.

Psalm 119:105 (NKJV) says, "Your word is a lamp to my feet and a light to my path." The Scriptures illuminate the darkness around us, showing us the way to go. The times in my life when I feel stuck, confused, or just directionless, I always turn to the Bible to give me fresh direction and insight as to where I should go next. I honestly can't comprehend how so many Christians survive so long without the Word of God lighting their path. I believe as the days get darker, we will need the Scripture more than ever before to show us the path to take.

4. Take up your cross daily and follow Jesus.

Luke 9:23 (NKJV) says, "Then He said to them all, 'If anyone desires to come after Me, let him deny himself, and take up his cross daily, and follow Me.'" One of the first commands Jesus gives anyone who wants to be His disciple is, "Deny yourself." This is the exact opposite of what you hear in most churches today. Most pastors preach about living your best life and giving in to your own wants and needs; nope, not Jesus. Jesus says it's not about you—deny you. The flesh is incredibly selfish and wicked, and all it thinks about is self, so it must be denied; it must be crucified. If you want to make sure demons don't return, this is something you must do daily. It's not enough that you pick up your cross only on Sunday morning for church service. You have to make it a daily activity. Every morning you get out of bed, you need to decide that today you will carry your cross and follow Jesus.

Jesus says, "Follow me"; He does not follow us. We have this backward. We basically do whatever we want and expect Jesus to follow us around. Sheep do not lead their shepherds. A shepherd leads the sheep. The best way to know if you're following Jesus is to see if you make your own decisions. If you make your own decisions, Jesus is following you; you're not following Him. True followers do not make a move unless Jesus says to. They follow His voice, they obey His commands, and they don't do anything unless He tells them to. Living in this way will ensure no demon reenters your life. How can a demon find an open door if you're following Christ daily? If you feel like you've been making Jesus follow you instead of you following Him, then pray this short prayer right now:

> *Jesus, I repent for doing my own thing. I am sorry for not following You as I should. Lord Jesus, please help me to follow You as the Good Shepherd. Help me every single day to deny my own desires and pick up my cross. Lord, from now on I will only do what You want me to do; I will follow Your voice and Your Spirit. Jesus, I am choosing today to say no to my flesh and say yes to You. You're my Master, You're my Lord, and I submit myself to Your will for my life. Amen.*

5. Get involved in a local church.

When a wolf attacks, its primary target is the sheep who is alone and isolated. A major key to maintaining your freedom and staying free from demonic infestation is to find a body of believers to walk alongside you. Hebrews 10:25 says, "And let us not neglect our meeting together, as some people do, but encourage one another, especially now that the day of his return is drawing near." Something powerful happens when the church comes together in unity. If you think about it in military terms, many of the armies in the world measure military power by how many soldiers they have. This is because there is power in numbers. It's why Jesus sent the disciples out together and not alone; it's why, over and over, you will see the disciples traveling together, praying together, eating together, and staying in community.

Ecclesiastes 4:9–12 (ESV) says,

> Two are better than one because they have a good reward for
> their toil. For if they fall, one will lift up his fellow. But woe
> to him who is alone when he falls and has not another to lift
> him up! Again, if two lie together, they keep warm, but how
> can one keep warm alone? And though a man might prevail
> against one who is alone, two will withstand him—a three-
> fold cord is not quickly broken.

Notice how Solomon, the writer of Ecclesiastes, says that
one of the main reasons two are better than one is that if one
person falls, there is someone to pick them up. Do your best to
surround yourself with people who will pick you up. Are you
hanging around people who bring you down or pick you up?
Demons would love to bring people into your life who cause you
to regress and not progress. It is your choice to surround yourself
with those who build you up, pick you up, and encourage you.
This is often found in the local church.

Spiritual growth is another important reason for involvement in a local church. The pastors and leaders will help train
and equip you to fight the good fight. In a church community,
you have opportunities for spiritual growth through teaching,
preaching, and discipleship. Ephesians 4:11–13 (ESV) tells us,

> And he gave the apostles, the prophets, the evangelists, the
> shepherds and teachers, to equip the saints for the work of
> ministry, for building up the body of Christ, until we all attain
> to the unity of the faith and of the knowledge of the Son of
> God, to mature manhood, to the measure of the stature of the
> fullness of Christ.

The key role of these ministry leaders is not to entertain you;
they are to equip you for the work of the ministry. Sadly, in the
Western church we are more entertainment driven than driven

to equip, but if we go back to the biblical blueprint, we will see the church is about equipping the saints.

Accountability is a valuable asset of being a part of the local church, especially if you have recently been delivered. Accountability is vital in maintaining that freedom. James 5:16 (esv) says, "Therefore, confess your sins to one another and pray for one another, that you may be healed. The prayer of a righteous person has great power as it is working." There are times when being able to find someone to confess your sins to is extremely powerful. Demons like to work under the cover of darkness; they want you to keep your sin a secret. James is challenging us to bring our sin to the light and expose it for what it really is. The result of you confessing your sin to a brother or sister is that a wave of healing comes, as James says, that you may be healed!

Let me give you one last valuable piece of advice about staying free after deliverance and why involvement in a local church is so important. Boredom is the devil's playground. When I'm dealing with people who have reopened the door to the enemy, they usually say it started with them being bored. When you're bored, your mind wanders, and your flesh capitalizes on that and entices you to reopen old doors.

One of the beauties of being involved in a local church is you get to stay busy. There is always a need in the local church that you can fill. The local church is a place where you can use your spiritual gifts to serve others and participate in ministry. First Peter 4:10 (esv) says, "As each has received a gift, use it to serve one another, as good stewards of God's varied grace." So we all have received a gift, and we should not be idle with it but instead use it. When you're so busy using your gift and serving those in the body of Christ, you will not even have time to be bored and start returning to old cycles of sin!

6. Develop a prayer life.

The last but not least way to ensure that demons don't return after your deliverance is to develop a strong prayer life. This goes back to what I mentioned earlier: A demon doesn't want to live with someone who is constantly praying! A famous saying goes something like this: "The more you pray, the harder it is to sin, and the more you sin, the harder it is to pray." After all, the more you spend time with God in prayer, the more you will become like Him. The more things you have in common with Jesus, the less you will have in common with darkness.

In John 14:30 (NKJV) Jesus said this about Satan: "I will no longer talk much with you, for the ruler of this world is coming, and he has nothing in Me." What gave Jesus complete authority over the enemy is that He and the enemy had nothing in common; Satan had no power *over* Jesus or *in* Jesus. It goes without saying that Jesus had the greatest prayer life in history. This was a man who, after a long day of ministry, would get away alone with the Father and pray all night. What a perfect model to follow.

> The more things you have in common with Jesus, the less you will have in common with darkness.

A key component to this is not just regular prayer but praying in the name of Jesus. Jesus said in John 16:23–24 (NKJV), "And in that day you will ask Me nothing. Most assuredly, I say to you, whatever you ask the Father in My name He will give you. Until now you have asked nothing in My name. Ask, and you will receive, that your joy may be full."

When we pray in the name of Jesus, we are coming to God not

in the power of what we have done but in the power of what Jesus did on the cross. Two times in this verse Jesus tells us the key to getting our prayers answered is asking in His name. He even tells the disciples that until this point they have asked nothing in His name. What a mistake we make when we expect God to answer prayers we are not even praying.

When we pray in His name, we are praying with His authority. Imagine if you had a friend who was a police officer, and one day you put on their uniform and went out to try to direct traffic. Even though you were not really an officer, and even though you never had the training, people would listen to you and respect you because of the uniform and badge. This is how it works when we put on Christ even though in ourselves we have no power or authority. We are not coming in our name; we are coming in His name and putting on His badge and His uniform. This is why demons have to obey us, because we come in His name and authority. When we pray, we have that level of authority.

When I pray in Jesus' name, I am declaring myself to have no power. It's like a bride who has no money but marries a rich man and takes on his name, and now everything he has becomes hers, and she goes from being poor and powerless to wealthy and influential just by changing her name.

Here are some powerful Scripture references you can study on your own where we see the name of Jesus being used:

- Luke 10:17—Demons are powerless because of His name.

- Mark 16:17—Demons are cast out in His name.

- Acts 3:6—Healing occurs in His name.

- Acts 4:12—Salvation comes in His name.

- Matthew 28:19—We are baptized in His name.

- 1 Corinthians 6:11—We are justified in His name.

- Colossians 3:17—Everything we do or say is done in His name.

Begin to develop a prayer life where you frequently pray in His name, and you will see immediate results. That is a promise from God's Word!

In summary, we know that demons are looking for an empty house to live in, so we must fill our houses (our lives) with the power and fruit of the Holy Spirit. If we want to keep the demons from returning, we must

1. keep the doors closed,

2. speak God's Word over our lives,

3. stay in the Scripture,

4. take up our cross daily and follow Jesus,

5. get involved in a local church, and

6. develop a prayer life.

If you make a practice of doing all six things I outlined in this chapter, you will be able to keep demons from reentering once and for all.

Chapter 10

AVOID THESE DELIVERANCE MISTAKES

ROM THE MOMENT I got called into the ministry, my uncle Ben, who is also my spiritual father and covering, would always tell me, "Isaiah, I made thirty years of ministry mistakes so you don't have to." He told me I could avoid years of wasted time and heartache if I would listen to his wisdom and guidance. This never made sense to me until he often warned me of things *not* to do in ministry. He would say, "Trust me, don't do that. I've already made that mistake."

I can honestly say that every time I listened to him, even if I didn't agree, it would always work out exactly as he said. I have avoided years of mistakes by learning from the mistakes he had already made. You can ignore others' mistakes and do it harder, or you can listen to the mistakes others have made, heed their wisdom, and do it smarter. A famous saying says those who do not learn from history are doomed to repeat it. Although this chapter is toward the end of this book, it is vital to be successful in deliverance ministry. I want to share with you seven mistakes I have made during my years of deliverance ministry so you can avoid them and save years of time. Let's start with the first and most common mistake.

1. Sticking to one specific method

As you grow in deliverance ministry, you will quickly realize no two deliverances are the same. Each one presents a unique set of challenges and circumstances. I often see the deliverance process as a puzzle, and as the deliverance progresses, you are putting it together piece by piece, trying to solve the bigger picture. There is no right or wrong order, as long as the puzzle gets solved. Maybe the demon won't leave, maybe the person has unresolved trauma or unforgiveness, maybe the demon refuses to talk or talks too much, or maybe the deliverance stalls out. These are all pieces that often need to be solved before you can move on in the deliverance process.

In the midst of that there are methods or strategies you can learn that are very effective. I laid out my seven-step method in chapter 7, but the important thing to understand is that no right method works every time, so we can't be dogmatic about our approach. A major mistake I have seen deliverance ministers make over the years is sticking to one method and refusing to deviate even if they are unsuccessful at getting people free. It's essential that we follow the leading of the Holy Spirit and not our specific methods.

In John 14:26 (ESV) Jesus said, "But the Helper, the Holy Spirit, whom the Father will send in my name, he will teach you all things and bring to your remembrance all that I have said to you." Notice that the Holy Spirit is the helper, not the doer. He is there to help you when doing the deliverance. He knows what the person needs, the hindrances and stumbling blocks, and the fastest and most effective route to setting people free. It will massively benefit you to follow His lead.

When I am doing deliverance, the Holy Spirit will often tell me what demons are there even before the demon or person reveals that information. When the demon tries to lie or mislead me, I don't take the bait because the Holy Spirit has already helped me by revealing the truth. He will constantly give you new strategies or different strategies depending on what demon you are dealing with, how demonized the person is, how strong the demon is, and what the deliverance setting is. Before I even ask the demon its name, I inquire of the Holy Spirit. If I don't feel the Holy Spirit revealing the information to me, or it seems like a struggle to hear what He is saying, I will try my own methods. At the end of the day if He tells you to do something that might conflict with a method a ministry taught you, obey the Holy Spirit!

I would highly caution you against judging the methods of other people who are getting results. It's very easy to look at another deliverance ministry and say they are doing it wrong simply because they're not doing it the way you're doing it. The disciples saw people casting out demons who were not in their group and told Jesus. Listen to what Jesus said to them:

> John said to Jesus, "Master, we saw someone using your name to cast out demons, but we told him to stop because he isn't in our group." But Jesus said, "Don't stop him! Anyone who is not against you is for you."
> —Luke 9:49

Jesus says, "Listen! Just because they're not in our group or doing it the way we do does not mean they are not of Me." Then He clarifies by saying they are for us if they are not against us. We must be careful not to persecute, slander, or bad-mouth other ministries because they differ from us. However, there is one group you want to avoid advice from, and whose strategies you want to avoid using, and that is those who don't practice deliverance.

A growing number of leaders in the body of Christ are teaching—or rather *trying* to teach—deliverance but don't actually practice deliverance ministry. The problem with this is that there are many things only the school of experience can teach you. You may believe one thing, but once you get into deliverance, you will realize you were wrong about what you believed, because your experience does not align with your philosophy. They will say things like, "Well, I don't let the demon manifest; I don't let the demon talk; for me, I get it done in five minutes." These things all sound great in theory but don't work in practice. The truth is that demons often manifest and often talk, and it usually takes a lot longer than five minutes. By saying that, all you've told me is that you have no experience.

Imagine a brain surgeon in the middle of surgery, and suddenly a janitor walks in to change the garbage bag. Do you think the brain surgeon will stop to ask the janitor for advice on the surgery? Of course not; it's not his field, and he has no experience. In the same way why would you take advice or counsel from someone without experience in the field? Football players don't stop in the middle of a game to take advice from people in the stands, and we should not stop doing deliverances to take advice from people with no experience in the field.

I believe it's time for the body of Christ to enlist in the school of experience. We have many Bible college professors who don't practice what they teach. I want to learn from people who do what they teach. So let's always follow the Holy Spirit's guidance and be willing to take advice from others, but be careful not to take advice from the wrong sources.

2. Trying to deliver someone who is not ready or willing

The person being delivered must be ready and willing to be set free for the demon to leave. Often family members will bring someone for deliverance who doesn't want it, and I usually tell them up front that this will not work. Both God and Satan recognize free will. In the same way you can't force someone to be saved, you can't force someone to get delivered. Demons recognize when the person does not want to be free and they have a legal right to stay no matter how many times you command them to leave in Jesus' name; they do not have to obey. As a deliverance minister, you should not spend precious time and resources trying to force someone to be delivered. Plenty of other people out there want it, and this is only a waste of time.

You might ask yourself, "Who comes for deliverance but doesn't want to be free?" I used to think the same thing until, time after time, I dealt with people who were more comfortable in bondage. Several years ago I was praying for a woman to be delivered, and it just seemed as if things were going nowhere. The demon was manifesting; she had dealt with unforgiveness and even renounced things that could have hindered her deliverance. Everything should

> Football players don't stop in the middle of a game to take advice from people in the stands, and we should not stop doing deliverances to take advice from people with no experience in the field.

have been going smoothly, but after two hours the Holy Spirit whispered, "She doesn't want to be free; she likes her demons." I thought to myself, "That is odd. Who likes their demons?"

Immediately I stopped and said, "I don't think this is going to work. This might sound weird, but are you afraid of them leaving? Do you like your demons?" She started crying hysterically and said, "I do like them! They've been with me so long I don't know how I will be without them. I just feel like they are so much a part of my personality." That is when I realized some people are actually in love with their demons and not ready or willing to be free.

Before I got saved, I was training to become a deputy sheriff, and in one of my college classes we learned about something called Stockholm syndrome. Stockholm syndrome is a theory that explains why hostages sometimes develop a psychological bond with their captors. This is something often developed in women who go through abuse—they fall in love with their abuser. The same goes for demons; although they torment, abuse, and try to destroy, some people fall in love with them.

Demons have a way of weaving themselves into their victims' minds and personalities, convincing them they are needed—even telling their victims they help them and love them. I have heard many people tell me their demons are not harmful. I have even had demons speak out of people, saying, "I'm not harming them; I'm not doing anything wrong." It might seem that way to the person, but nothing could be further from the truth. Demons are evil in nature. They do not understand or comprehend love. They are evil, vile spirits, and we must not believe this lie. My advice to you would be do not waste your time doing a deliverance on someone who doesn't truly want to be free. I tell people, "If I want you to be free more than you want to be free, this will not work."

3. Giving up early

I see this mistake all the time, especially with people new to deliverance. Many people fail to realize how much time, energy,

Avoid These Deliverance Mistakes

and commitment it takes to stay with someone until they are free. There is a common lie that deliverance should be fast. People only think that because they say, "Well, Jesus did it fast," to which I respond, "You're not Jesus. We are His students and ambassadors." Everyone Jesus prayed for was healed, but that doesn't mean everyone we pray for will be healed. Now, of course, I would like every deliverance to be fast. Nobody wants to spend hours dealing with a stubborn demon, but the reality is that often it takes a long time, and that's OK.

The fact is people have spent years opening doors to demons, entertaining demons, and feeding their demons yet expect them all to leave in minutes. It's just not the case. A doctor does not rush a surgery because it "should" be fast; he takes his time and is precise and thorough to ensure the job gets done. This is the mentality we need in approaching a deliverance session.

Demons are professionals at making you waste time. They waste time to prolong the deliverance so you will give up. The mindset you need to have going into a deliverance is "I am going to last longer than this demon; I am not leaving until this person is free." One time I was going to pray for someone to be delivered, and before we walked in the door, I told my team outside, "Guys, let's get this done in about an hour because we have a church prayer meeting at 6 p.m." The time when we walked in was 4 p.m.

We started the deliverance, and things were going great. We were a little over an hour in, and I started getting nervous because I had to be back to lead the prayer meeting, but I didn't want to tell the demon or the person being delivered I had to leave, as I knew the demon would use that against me. Finally, I told the demon, "Why are you so stubborn! Why won't you leave?" To my surprise the demon said, "You have to leave in a few minutes; I'm going to outlast you." I was shocked, and so was my team. I never

155

even said this around the person, yet somehow the demon knew I had to go.

Often to discourage you into giving up, they will say things like, "I am too strong for you," or, "This person is not going to get free today," or, "You can't help them; I'm not leaving." The problem is that even if you aren't convinced of these lies, the person who is going through the deliverance will often get convinced and begin to doubt. You must reassure them, "You will be set free today!" Don't let the demon's lies stop you from pressing through. Don't let the lies stop you from staying with the person until they are free. After all, this is warfare.

> Do not waste your time doing a deliverance on someone who doesn't truly want to be free.

Deliverance takes an incredible amount of energy for the person doing it and the person receiving it. Usually when I get done with a deliverance, I'm dead tired. Mark 6:31 (NIV) says, "Then, because so many people were coming and going that they did not even have a chance to eat, he said to them, 'Come with me by yourselves to a quiet place and get some rest.'" The demand is so great that often there is no time for food, breaks, or rest. Sometimes you must seize the moment and push through until they are free. There is always time to eat and rest later; fasting a meal won't kill you.

Patience is another attribute you need in deliverance ministry. Some do not always retain their deliverance and need follow-up prayer or help. It is very easy to get frustrated with these people and even reject their requests, but I must remind myself how patient Jesus has been with me. God has been so kind and patient with me, and it is only right for me to extend that grace to those I minister to. Some are slow and must continually be told the same thing or encouraged.

There is a temptation to spend time with others who show more fruit, but we must be patient with slow learners. We used to call these people EGR, which stands for "extra grace required." Some people require more grace than others, and that's OK.

4. Not utilizing spiritual weapons

God has given us supernatural weapons to use in deliverance, so why wouldn't we use them? No soldier goes into battle without his weapon, and no deliverance minister should go into deliverance without fully utilizing all the weapons at our disposal. Second Corinthians 10:4 (NIV) says, "The weapons we fight with are not the weapons of the world. On the contrary, they have divine power to demolish strongholds."

I hope you caught that. We do not fight demons with natural weapons, such as a sniper rifle or a pistol. These are supernatural weapons to defeat supernatural enemies. I will not be too exhaustive on this (see Ephesians 6:10–17 for more on the armor of God), but let's talk about a few weapons that rarely get used in deliverance.

Using the name of Jesus is the most powerful weapon in our arsenal. Always use His name in deliverance ministry. I see people commanding demons to leave but not doing it in the name of Jesus. *This is a huge mistake!* There is no power in my name or your name; there is only power and authority in the name of Jesus. Ephesians 1:21–22 says,

> Now he is far above any ruler or authority or power or leader or anything else—not only in this world but also in the world to come. God has put all things under the authority of Christ and has made him head over all things for the benefit of the church.

Jesus is far above the demonic powers we fight, and when we use His name, we exercise the authority He has given us over demonic spirits.

The power of agreement is another spiritual weapon often not utilized. Matthew 18:19 (NKJV) says, "Again I say to you that if two of you agree on earth concerning anything that they ask, it will be done for them by My Father in heaven." Sometimes when a deliverance stalls out, I will have the prayer team all agree and command the demon out in one voice; there is great victory in this strategy. Demons hate when Christians agree with one another. They will do everything they can to divide the deliverance team because they know the power of unity and agreement.

Spiritual gifts are also vital in deliverance. For some reason, many people don't realize they can use the spiritual gifts God has given them when doing deliverance. The three main ones you will use are (1) word of knowledge, specifically when deliverance stalls out and you need God to reveal why or maybe the name of the next demon; (2) word of wisdom, for when you're making decisions and trying to devise a battle plan; and (3) discerning of spirits, to discern which spirits are in the person and how they function. This is also vital in discerning what the Holy Spirit is doing in the deliverance. We have so many powerful weapons available to us. Why wouldn't we use them all?

5. Lacking faith

Deliverance is not "Let's try this out and see what happens." You have to have 100 percent conviction that the person you're praying for will get free. You need *faith* when it comes to deliverance ministry. Many people go into it not being convinced it will work, and if that is your mindset, you have lost the battle before it has even begun. It is incredibly important that the person doing the deliverance has faith, as well as the person getting delivered.

The man who brought his son to the disciples to be healed in

Matthew 17:16 (NIV) told Jesus, "I brought him to your disciples, but they could not heal him." The Lord spoke to me one day and said, "Isaiah, on judgment day, the world will come to Me and say, 'We brought our demonized, our sick, and our hurting to Your people, but Your people did not help them.'" Sadly, we are giving people everything else in the church but healing and deliverance; it is our obligation, responsibility, and mandate to heal those who are sick and deliver those who are demonized. We are giving them programs, good light shows, and concerts, but we are failing to bring the supernatural power of God to people. So many churches and Christians have a form of godliness but deny the power of God. People are coming to us for help. Don't be like these disciples who couldn't help the young boy.

> No soldier goes into battle without his weapon, and no deliverance minister should go into deliverance without fully utilizing all the weapons at our disposal.

This goes for every believer. Deliverance is not for the special or unique; it's for every believer to do according to Mark 16:17. Jesus replied to the man, saying, "O faithless and perverse generation" (Matt. 17:17, NKJV). Jesus calls them faithless, which means untrustworthy. Jesus is saying, "I have given you this power and authority, and I can't even trust you to use it; I can't even trust you to apply it properly. You guys still don't realize the authority and power you have." The father of the boy is not exempt. Jesus is speaking to the entire crowd. In deliverance make sure you don't have those with no faith present. Sometimes the person will bring a friend or family member, but they don't believe in deliverance ministry. Ensure they are not in the room because their faith can also affect the deliverance.

The father's response in Mark 9:22 (NKJV) was, "If You can do anything, have compassion on us and help us," and Jesus responded, "What do you mean, 'If I can'?...Anything is possible if a person believes." The man's *if* was a sign of his unbelief. Some people will say, "*If* you can help me, I want deliverance." What do you mean by *if*? There can't be any *ifs* in our minds; we have to be convinced that God will set the captives free! You need to get it out of your vocabulary and say, "God can and will do this! I am sure of it!"

So the failed deliverance was due not only to the disciples' but the religious people's lack of faith. It was also due to the boy's father's lack of faith. Matthew 13:58 says Jesus did not do many works there because of their unbelief. Unbelief shuts down the miracle power of God from flowing. No wonder God isn't moving in so many churches; they don't even believe in miracles and deliverance. So many people don't believe in deliverance because they haven't seen it and don't realize that is why they haven't seen it! The world teaches you to see it to believe it; the Bible teaches you to believe it, and then you will see it. People say their pastor believes in it, but if they don't do it themselves, then they don't believe. Don't try telling me you believe in healing but don't pray for the sick, or believe in deliverance but don't do it. You say you believe in the baptism of the Spirit but don't pray for it. I'm not buying it.

The man's response to Jesus is recorded in Mark 9:24 (NKJV): "Immediately the father of the child cried out and said with tears, 'Lord, I believe; help my unbelief!'" This should be our prayer: "Lord, help my unbelief so that I can recognize my unbelief." You need to recognize it and repent of it. Ask the Lord right now to help your unbelief.

6. Extra-biblical or anti-biblical methods

Sadly, there is a lot of abuse regarding deliverance ministry. Most people throw the baby out with the bathwater, but this is an error. Just because people abuse deliverance with extra-biblical or anti-biblical methods does not mean we should be negative toward deliverance. One of the extra-biblical methods I've heard recently that is completely wrong is you must give money to be set free. This is a sad abuse that is not scriptural; not only is this extra-biblical, but it is also anti-biblical.

In Matthew 10:7–8 (NIV) Jesus says, "As you go, proclaim this message: 'The kingdom of heaven has come near.' Heal the sick, raise the dead, cleanse those who have leprosy, drive out demons. Freely you have received; freely give." Notice Jesus uses the world *freely*. There is no price attached to your breakthrough. I am specifically talking about requiring someone to give money, or they won't be set free. That is not biblical. Deliverance is a free gift for which Christ already paid the price. Never in Scripture was someone commanded to give so the demons would come out. Never in Scripture was money attached to demons coming out. Don't get me wrong; giving our finances does a lot of positive things in our lives, but receiving deliverance is not one of them.

Another method that is flat-out wrong is when deliverance gets turned into a show. Deliverance is not a show. It's a miracle, and it should not be exploited or used for social media growth or likes and views. It's one thing to show a deliverance video to build faith and encourage others to participate. It is quite another thing when you put on a show mocking the demon and the person being delivered. This is wrong and degrading. People should never be mocked or exploited during deliverance ministry.

They should be loved, covered, and protected, as this is one of the most vulnerable moments of their lives.

Although Christ did deliverance in public for the crowds to see, He handled people with compassion. Making the person do embarrassing things and mocking their demons is wrong and sadly common in many deliverance ministries. Demons should never be mocked. Jude 9 (NIV) says, "But even the archangel Michael, when he was disputing with the devil about the body of Moses, did not himself dare to condemn him for slander but said, 'The Lord rebuke you!'" Jude makes it clear that even Michael did not slander Satan during their warfare. We should not be mocking demons.

7. Talking to the demon too much

This is a rookie mistake I will admit to making in my early days. When you're engaged in warfare and the demon begins to divulge information, it gets tempting to ask questions that are not necessary. Once demons start talking, they usually love to keep talking to divert and distract the deliverance. If you rely too much on what the demon is telling you, or you rely too much on their information, you will allow them to direct the deliverance. The Holy Spirit should be guiding you, not the demons. Do not let your strategy of attack be led by the information you got from demons but instead by the Holy Spirit. I've had times when a demon would tell me something, causing me to change my strategy, and after two hours of wasted time I realized all they were doing was diverting my attention and getting me off track.

Allowing the demon to talk too much also prolongs the deliverance and is insensitive to the person being delivered. As long as a demon can distract you, he prolongs his eviction notice. It's like a tenant who can't pay rent and is begging for another week. This is what happens when we converse too long with demons. Also, it's exhausting and confusing for the person. Oftentimes the person is in physical pain and sore in the end. Demons can be extremely violent. So this begs the question "How long should you talk to demons during a deliverance?"

First, let me be clear: I am not against asking a demon for its name or interrogating it, but remember, it's interrogation, not conversation. If you start asking the demon about unrelated things, you know you've gone too long. In my early days I can recall a deliverance where the demon was saying a group of witches was coming to our revival meeting to try to shut it down. This led my team and me down a rabbit hole for over an hour, questioning the demon to get information on these witches, which led to a dead end and a waste of time. We talked too long.

There are helpful reasons to talk to a demon during deliverance. Usually, if you can't figure out why a demon won't leave, you can ask them their name and why they are still there. Oftentimes because they are in pain (deliverance is torment to demons), they will give you the information you need. The information or name can be used against them when trying to drive them out. I've lost track of how many times in deliverance the information the demon gave was actually the key to getting the person delivered.

The bottom line is that deliverance ministry is hard and often messy. Many people would rather just not get involved to avoid the mess. But that's like saying I don't want to have a baby because giving birth is messy. There may be a mess at the time of delivery, but the end result is beautiful, and you don't even remember the mess after the baby comes. If you take heed to what I have explained in this chapter, it will help clear up a lot of the mess and make deliverance a lot smoother and easier to walk in. Like my uncle Ben always told me, I made the mistakes so you don't have to! Trust me when I say I have made every mistake I've listed in this chapter, and that's OK. Learn from my mistakes so you can avoid them.

Chapter 11

DEMOLISHING MENTAL STRONGHOLDS

B REAKING FREE FROM the chains that bind our minds is crucial in the journey of casting out demons. As believers we often face mental strongholds—deeply ingrained patterns of thinking that keep us from experiencing the fullness of God's freedom. Romans 12:2 (NIV) urges us, "Do not conform to the pattern of this world but be transformed by the renewing of your mind. Then you will be able to test and approve what God's will is—his good, pleasing, and perfect will." By renewing our minds with God's truth, we can demolish these strongholds, remove the footholds demons exploit, and walk in the freedom and authority that Christ has given us. An unseen battle is going on in the mind that must be understood to live a life of lasting freedom.

The main battlefield for most people is not in the spiritual realm but in the mind. The danger of this war that takes place in the mind is that it is easy to hide from the people around you.

When you're fighting addiction, most of the people around you know it; when you're fighting demonic spirits, most of the people around you know it. Exterior struggles are easy to discern, but this battle is much different, as it takes place in an area that's easy to hide from others. The battle that goes on in the mind is a very complex thing, a labyrinth of thoughts and emotions that is often misunderstood and underestimated. People often battle in their minds for years before having a breakdown, and then the people around them say, "I didn't even realize they were going through this!" That's because the battle was happening in secret.

MENTAL FORTRESSES

Mental strongholds are fortresses the enemy builds in our minds to keep us trapped in cycles of sin and wrong thinking patterns. These strongholds are often easy to identify, as they manifest as persistent issues or thoughts we can't seem to overcome. Even after experiencing deliverance from a demon, being born again, and serving God passionately, we may still struggle with these mental barriers. These lingering struggles are what we refer to as strongholds.

> The main battlefield for most people is not in the spiritual realm but in the mind.

Another way to think about it is that the devil has a stronghold on you. It may feel as if anxiety is gripping you, and you succumb to it. Maybe it's fear; maybe it's depression; maybe it's irrational thoughts. These are mental strongholds. It all starts with lies that Satan plants in our minds, which we believe as truth, even though they are not. When we listen to these lies and accept them as reality, a stronghold is established. These strongholds are usually built over time, but they can also arise from traumatic experiences.

I began learning about mental strongholds when I encountered people who believed they had demons. They would go through deliverance, but nothing would manifest. I found myself puzzled, thinking, "If this isn't a demon, what is it?" The problem was that they continued in wrong thinking patterns, remaining bound by toxic emotions and mindsets. I realized that something deeper was at play—something that wasn't a demon, a curse, or merely a battle with the flesh. For many their thought life was something they would be horrified for others to know about. If our thoughts were projected onto a screen for all to see, it would be shocking. Thankfully, we are not judged by our thoughts alone but by our actions. However, our thoughts often turn into actions, and many people give in to their thoughts because they don't understand how to find mental freedom. God desires that we be free not just spiritually but also mentally.

Strongholds are often issues we've struggled with for years, and the longer they've been there, the harder they seem to be to destroy because they've been built up over time. It's like a castle that someone adds bricks to every week; after several years (or even decades) it becomes massive and difficult to demolish. To tear it down, you'd need some powerful equipment. Thankfully, we have the most powerful weapons in existence: God's Word and God's power. Second Corinthians 10:3–6 (NKJV) says,

> For though we walk in the flesh, we do not war according to the flesh. For the weapons of our warfare are not carnal but mighty in God for pulling down strongholds, casting down arguments and every high thing that exalts itself against the knowledge of God, bringing every thought into captivity to the obedience of Christ, and being ready to punish all disobedience when your obedience is fulfilled.

Although we walk in the flesh, we go to war in the spirit. The good news is that in this war we have weapons—powerful spiritual weapons—at our disposal.

The first thing Paul charges us to do is cast down our imaginations. Imagination involves forming new ideas, concepts, and principles. We get in trouble when we create doctrines or ideas in our minds that violate God's Word but accept them as right. For example, we may think, "I can do this wrong thing but still serve God," or, "I can watch this but still be holy," or, "I can serve God on Sundays, live carnally all week, and still be faithful," or, "I can pick and choose from God's Word." These are all imaginations we've created. Recognizing their error is the first step. Then we must cast these things down. Part of this process is repenting, which is changing the way we think and turning from our sinful ways.

Next we must destroy arguments and opinions against the knowledge of God and take every thought captive. This speaks directly to the mind. Be cautious not to go down rabbit holes, learning about demonic doctrines that create strongholds. Taking thoughts captive is essential. I will discuss later how to consecrate and purify our thoughts, but for now, notice the language Paul uses: Take the thoughts captive, bind the thoughts, arrest the thoughts. These thoughts are like wild animals that must be caged and tied up. If you don't, they will run wild and cause damage to your life.

Psalm 94:19 (AMP) says, "When my anxious thoughts multiply within me, your comforts delight me." Can anyone relate to what David is talking about? We all experience those loops of thought where the more you think about something, the more anxious you become. You might start with a small concern, like noticing a spot on your body, and ten minutes later you're worrying if it's cancer and if you're going to die. Or you might start thinking about the economy, and before you know it, you're worried about losing your job, your home, and everything you've worked so hard for. The longer you dwell on these thoughts, the more they multiply. That's why it's crucial to bind them and capture them before they get out of control.

All of us are made of three parts: our physical bodies, our spirits, and our souls. Our physical bodies are what other people see when they look at us. Our spirits are where God dwells when we repent and are born again. Our souls comprise our minds, wills, and emotions. When we are born again, God breathes His Spirit—the Holy Spirit—into us, and our spirits become alive. We were created to then "walk in the Spirit," meaning we submit our bodies, minds, wills, and emotions to the Spirit of God, who is now alive in us. The more we allow the Holy Spirit to move in our lives, the more our minds, wills, and emotions are transformed.

Suddenly, I want to do things for God—that's my will being renewed and changed by God's power. My mind no longer dwells on earthly things but on things above. I stop thinking of lustful things and plotting against people, and instead of seeing the worst in people, I begin to see the best in them—that's my mind being renewed. Emotions are a huge area of transformation because many of us have damaged emotions from childhood trauma, life experiences, letdowns, and toxic relationships.

I remember not crying for nearly ten years. My heart was so hard, and my emotions were so messed up. But when I encountered God, I bawled like a baby. Now I can be in prayer, start crying, and not even know why. This is God restoring and renewing my emotions.

First Thessalonians 5:23 (KJV) explains this beautifully: "May the very God of peace sanctify you completely. And I pray to God that your whole spirit, soul, and body be preserved blameless unto the coming of our Lord Jesus Christ." The Greek word translated as "completely" in this verse is *holoteles*, meaning "perfect, complete in all respects."[1] Think about this: Paul is praying that we reach a point where our souls are undamaged and perfect, complete and whole through and through. This is God's will for our lives, or Paul wouldn't be praying it. God doesn't want you to be damaged; you're not damaged goods. You might say, "Isaiah, I'm emotionally damaged from a relationship." You're in a perfect position for God to heal you. He wants you to be undamaged. This is the God we serve—He is a God who makes all things new.

Ephesians 4:22–24 (AMP) illustrates Paul's powerful message:

> Strip yourselves of your former nature [put off and discard your old unrenewed self] which characterized your previous manner of life and becomes corrupt through lusts and desires that spring from delusion; and be constantly renewed in the spirit of your mind [having a fresh mental and spiritual attitude], and put on the new nature (the regenerate self) created in God's image, [Godlike] in true righteousness and holiness.

To walk in personal victory over mental strongholds, we must lay down our old selves, strip off our sinful nature, and disarm the evil lusts, desires, and thoughts of the flesh. Paul emphasizes that we must actively participate in this process; we can't just sit back and expect it to happen automatically. You may think, "Well, this is God's will." But the truth is, you need to put effort into stripping off the old sinful nature.

The world continually tries to impose its ways on us while God calls us to keep stripping them off. It's not a one-time event; it's a constant process of shedding the influences the world tries to impose on us. God wants to restore, renew, and cleanse your thought life completely. To get more specific, let me outline a few mental strongholds that are most prevalent in this generation.

The stronghold of anxiety and fear

Anxiety, by definition, is the body's response to stress and fear. With so many of us juggling a multitude of responsibilities, there's always something to worry about. What if things go wrong? What if they don't go as planned? What if this? What if that? Worry only serves to fuel the flames of anxiety. Interestingly, the word *worry* stems from an Old English term meaning strangle. It's an apt description, as many of us have felt as though the worries of life have choked the passion, vitality, time, and energy out of us. Those bound by fear often find themselves living to please others, unable to fulfill the unique destiny God has designed for them.

Freedom from this cycle only comes when we shift our focus from worrying about people's opinions to caring about what God thinks. As 2 Timothy 1:7 (NKJV) says, "For God has not given us a spirit of fear, but of power and of love and of a sound mind." Fear and anxiety create noise and chaos in the mind, but God desires to bring peace and clarity. One strategy that has helped me overcome anxiety is to focus solely on today. Jesus speaks to this in Matthew 6:34 (BSB): "Therefore do not worry about tomorrow, for tomorrow will worry about itself. Today has enough trouble of its own." It's important to understand that most of the things you're afraid of happening will never actually happen. When you come to this realization and allow the peace of God to flood your mind, you will begin to get freedom from this stronghold.

The stronghold of sexual immorality

Sexual immorality has assaulted our generation, mainly through the advent of smartphones. The statistics on pornography use reveal how it has imprisoned many:

- One out of five mobile searches are for pornography.

- $3,075.64 is spent on porn every second on the internet.

- Over forty million Americans regularly visit porn sites.

- Twenty-eight thousand users are watching porn every second.

- 71 percent of teens hide their online behavior from their parents.

- One out of five youth pastors and one out of seven senior pastors use porn on a regular basis and currently are struggling. That's more than fifty thousand US church leaders.[2]

It's time to break free from this bondage. Solomon says in Ecclesiastes 7:26,

> I discovered that a seductive woman is a trap more bitter than death. Her passion is a snare, and her soft hands are chains. Those who are pleasing to God will escape her, but sinners will be caught in her snare.

Here, lust is described as complete and total bondage. It's important to see lust for what it really is. Colossians 3:5 (ESV) says, "Put to death therefore what is earthly in you," and the first thing Paul says to kill is sexual immorality. You have to kill this lust before it kills you. Lust seeks to destroy and wreak havoc on every area of your life. James 1:14–15 (ESV) warns, "Each person is tempted when he is lured and enticed by his own desires. Then, when desire is conceived, it gives birth to sin, and sin, when it is full-grown, gives birth to death." Lust's child is death.

Galatians 5:19–21 says that sexual impurity is a work of the flesh, and those who do such things will not inherit the kingdom of God. This is no joke; this is not a game. This is not just some website you visit or some pictures you send—this is your life on the line, your eternity at stake. God wants to bring down the stronghold of sexual immorality. If you have unwanted thoughts of sexual acts, if you think about sleeping with other people's spouses, if you continually struggle with pornography and hate it every time you finish, if you dwell on sexual fantasies or struggle with masturbation—these are all signs of a stronghold of lust in your mind. It's time to break free and let God restore purity and wholeness in your life.

The stronghold of trauma

I want to address trauma and tormenting thoughts, which can develop into strongholds. Tormenting thoughts often stem from traumatic experiences. Many of us have faced traumatic events in our lives and still deal with the residual effects, which usually manifest as tormenting thoughts. People who have undergone certain traumatic events can attest that their minds are never the same. In fact, a lot of mental illness originates from traumatic experiences. Satan does not play fair, and he uses these experiences to wreak havoc on our minds. Often these experiences become open doors for him to come in and torment us. When you get tormenting thoughts, do not dwell on them but take them captive so they don't become strongholds.

According to the *Merriam-Webster* dictionary, *trauma* is derived from the Greek word for *wound*. Although the Greeks used the term only for physical injuries, nowadays *trauma* is just as likely to refer to emotional wounds. We now know that a traumatic event can leave psychological symptoms long after any physical injuries have healed. The psychological reaction to emotional trauma now has an established name: post-traumatic stress disorder (PTSD). PTSD usually occurs after an extremely stressful event, such as wartime combat, a natural disaster, or sexual or physical abuse. Its symptoms include depression, anxiety, flashbacks, and recurring nightmares. Recognizing and addressing these tormenting thoughts can prevent them from becoming strongholds in our minds. God wants to bring healing and restoration to our minds, freeing us from the chains of trauma and torment.

I want you to know today that no matter what trauma you have experienced, Christ wants to bring healing and wholeness to your mind. Despite the plans, schemes, and traps of Satan, the finished work of the cross has the power to remove and eradicate every tormenting thought and traumatic stronghold completely. God is fighting for you and is ready to wash and cleanse your mind. Let me give you some practical steps to demolish mental strongholds.

1. Spend time with the Holy Spirit.

You become like those you spend time with. When you spend time with the Holy Spirit, He goes in and destroys strongholds in your life. Conversely, the less time you spend with Him, the less like Him you will be. You are who you hang out with, and if you want to see your future, look at the people you surround yourself with. As you spend time in prayer, you will—often without realizing it—take on the mind of Christ. The only way to know His mind is to hear His voice, which happens in prayer. Your old patterns of thinking will be replaced by God's thoughts. The longer you spend with someone, the more you start thinking like them, talking like them, and acting like them.

Many of us spend little to no time with the Holy Spirit and then wonder why we aren't more like Him. Schedule time if you have to; get alone with Him. Invite Him into the activities of your day. The Holy Spirit likes to be invited. Jesus went to the wedding banquet because He was invited—don't expect Him to come without an invitation. If you are going to work, say, "Holy

Spirit, I invite You." If you are going to school, say, "Holy Spirit, I invite You." In your home invite Him in. Make it a practice in your life to invite and host the presence of God. Be aware of Him throughout the day. Acknowledge His presence by saying, "I recognize You are here," or, "I appreciate Your presence." You don't have to pray in tongues all day—this is a relationship. Sometimes just sitting in someone's presence is enough because you love them.

It's impossible to spend time with Him and not change. You might find yourself saying, "I don't want to watch porn anymore," or, "I don't want to be angry anymore." You may no longer feel anxious, depressed, bitter,

> **The only way to undo wrong thinking is to cultivate right thinking.**

or resentful. We have access to someone the world does not have access to—He is our peace, our helper, our rest, our refuge in the storm. Don't limit your encounters with Him to Sundays. If that's the only time you seek Him, you're missing out on the richness of a daily relationship with the Holy Spirit. Make a habit of seeking Him every day, inviting Him into every part of your life, and watch as He transforms you from the inside out.

2. Speak and listen to God's Word.

The only way to undo wrong thinking is to cultivate right thinking. Jesus fought the devil with "It is written," wielding the sword of the Spirit with His words. We need to do the same by memorizing Scripture so that when the enemy comes, we can defeat him quickly. You won't always have time to look things up.

Romans 12:2 (NASB) says, "Do not be conformed to this world, but be transformed by the renewing of your mind, so that you may prove what the will of God is, that which is good and acceptable and perfect." Strongholds exist in the mind, and the renewing of the mind breaks them. What does it mean to be transformed? It means to be changed into the likeness of Christ. This transformation doesn't occur in our physical appearance. God isn't trying to make us look physically like Jesus; He is working to change our inner character and life into the likeness of Christ. How does this happen? Through the renewing of our minds—changing our way of thinking. God makes us think the way He thinks through His Word.

The Bible reveals God's way of thinking. If you want to know God's perspective on money, adultery, theft, cheating, jealousy, selfishness, humility, pride, or any other matter, read the Bible. The answers are there. When Jesus came to earth, He was called the Word of God. We are told that the Word became flesh. This means that if you want to know what God thinks about anything, look at the life of Jesus, and you will have the answer.

God wants us to embody His Word so that others can see it in us. Second Corinthians 3:2–3 (AMP) says,

> You are our letter [of recommendation], written in our hearts, known and read by everyone. You show that you are a letter from Christ, delivered by us, written not with ink but with the Spirit of the living God, not on tablets of stone but on tablets of human hearts.

People are reading our lives!

To break strongholds, listen to the Word of God. Practically speaking, turn on an audio Bible or listen to sermons. Many people have said, "Isaiah, your sermons have completely changed the way I think." They say, "So many strongholds in my mind have been broken through listening to God's Word preached." By immersing yourself in God's Word—both speaking and listening—you will begin to see a transformation in your life. Your thoughts will align more with God's thoughts, and the strongholds that once held you captive will be destroyed.

3. Confess your sins to God and others.

First John 1:9 (NKJV) says, "If we confess our sins, He is faithful and just to forgive us our sins and to cleanse us from all unrighteousness." The condition for forgiveness is first confessing our sins, admitting they're wrong, acknowledging our need for forgiveness, and deciding not to continue with them. So why wouldn't we just confess? The main reason is pride. Many people don't believe they are wrong or are unwilling to confront the fact that they are in sin. Most people could be instantly

> If you want to know what God thinks about anything, look at the life of Jesus, and you will have the answer.

forgiven if they recognized their true state. Unfortunately, the "American cupcake gospel" often fails to show us our true state of sin and depravity.

The Holy Spirit brings illumination and conviction, making us feel the weight of our sin. This conviction draws us to Christ, not away from Him.

Confession is not merely admission or saying, "I'm sorry." The original word for *confess* means "to say the same thing" or "agree."[3] This means that confession is me agreeing with God, seeing my actions, my sins, and my compromises the way God sees them. It involves viewing everything—movies, music, relationships—the way God sees it. In confession I align my perspective with God's perspective on my actions. James 5:16 (NIV) instructs, "Therefore confess your sins to each other and pray for each other so that you may be healed. The prayer of a righteous person is powerful and effective." The devil thrives in the darkness. When you expose him by confessing your sins to others, he loses his ability to continue building that specific stronghold in your life.

By confessing our sins to God and others, we bring light to the darkness and dismantle the enemy's strongholds. This practice of confession helps us receive forgiveness, healing, and ultimately freedom from the bondage of sin.

4. Make fasting a part of your life.

The Old Testament word for *fast* is *tsuwm*, which literally means to cover the mouth.[4] This implies that no food is consumed during a fast. Think about it: Nothing can go in if you cover your mouth. Similarly, when you fast, nothing should enter your mouth. This act of abstaining from food is a physical expression of seeking spiritual nourishment and cleansing.

In Matthew 6 Jesus names three practices that believers should engage in: "When you pray...when you give...when you fast" (Matt. 6:2, 5, 16, NIV). Notice He says "when," not "if." This signifies that every believer is called to pray, give, and fast. Fasting brings numerous spiritual benefits. It is an act of setting ourselves aside solely for the Lord and teaches us to deny our flesh so we can receive more of God. Fasting empowers our prayers and increases our spiritual discernment. It positions us to hear and recognize God's heart, voice, and timing more clearly. By denying our flesh, fasting brings us to a greater level of humility. Our faith is increased as we discover that we do not live by bread alone. Fasting positions us to see victory in battles and in seemingly impossible situations. When we fast, we experience breakthroughs against darkness.

One of the physical benefits of fasting is that it helps remove toxins and impurities from the body. When you stop eating, your body starts to look for food from within, consuming toxins and stored waste accumulated from unhealthy eating habits. This is why even people who are not religious will fast for health reasons. But fasting does more than cleanse your body; it also purifies you spiritually. When you fast, God begins to clear out all the spiritual toxins that have entered your life through movies, music, culture, and various experiences. He cleanses and washes you during fasting. As you deny your flesh, your spirit gains strength and begins to take control.

The Bible provides various examples of fasting durations:

One-day or partial-day fasts: Judges 20:26; 1 Samuel 7:6; 2 Samuel 1:12; 3:35; Nehemiah 9:1; Jeremiah 36:6

A one-night fast: Daniel 6:18–24

Three-day fasts: Esther 4:16; Acts 9:9

Seven-day fasts: 1 Samuel 31:13; 2 Samuel 12:16–23

A fourteen-day fast: Acts 27:33–34

A twenty-one-day fast: Daniel 10:3–13

Forty-day fasts: Deuteronomy 9:9; 1 Kings 19:8; Matthew 4:2

Fasts of unspecified lengths: Matthew 9:14; Luke 2:37; Acts 13:2; 14:23

These examples show that fasting can vary in length, and you can choose a duration that aligns with your spiritual goals and convictions.

Start small, but be intentional. Fasting may begin with a single meal or a day, but the impact it has on your spiritual life can be profound. Make fasting a regular part of your walk with God, and watch as He brings transformation and victory into your life.

5. Spend time thinking about good things.

Philippians 4:8 encourages us: "Finally, brothers, whatever is true, whatever is honest, whatever is just, whatever is pure, whatever is lovely, whatever is of good report, if there is any virtue, and if there is any praise, think on these things." What are we thinking about? We need to think about good things intentionally.

The Greek word for *think* here implies a concentrated, focused effort. Paul is telling us to fix our minds on things that reflect and reveal the nature of God.

Don't let your mind wander aimlessly. Notice that the first thing Paul says to think about is what is true. The Greek word for *true* is *alēthēs*, which means real, truthful, honest, and having integrity.[5] The problem is that many of us focus not on what is true, real, and honest but on things that worry and concern us. To experience peace and reflect God's character, we must make a concentrated effort to focus our thoughts on what is true and positive, aligning our minds with God's truth.

A study conducted by Dr. Walter Calvert and funded by the National Science Foundation revealed some startling statistics about human worry:

- 30 percent of our worries are about events in the past.

- 40 percent of the things we worry about never happen.

- 12 percent of our worries are unfounded health concerns.

- 10 percent of our worries are over minor and trivial issues.

- Only 8 percent of our worries are about real, legitimate issues.[6]

Why is this the case? Because Satan is a liar; he wants to fill our minds with untrue things. Imagine the hours we spend worrying about things that will never happen or are not true. We need to choose to think about good things. By intentionally focusing our minds on positive and truthful thoughts, we can break free from the cycle of unnecessary worry and align ourselves more closely with God's truth.

As we wrap up this chapter on demolishing mental strongholds, remember that breaking free from the chains that bind our minds is essential for experiencing true freedom in Christ. These strongholds often develop from persistent issues or traumatic experiences, but by identifying and addressing them, we can start to dismantle them. We can overcome these barriers with the power of God's Word, the guidance of the Holy Spirit, and practical steps such as prayer, fasting, and renewing our minds.

Second Corinthians 10:4–5 tells us, "The weapons we fight with are not the weapons of the world. On the contrary, they have divine power to demolish strongholds." By consistently applying these spiritual principles, we can align our thoughts with God's truth, break free from the enemy's lies, and walk in the freedom and authority Christ has given us. True transformation begins in the mind, and with God's help you can live a life of lasting freedom and victory. Remember, you're not alone in this journey—God is with you every step of the way, ready to help you break down these strongholds and live a life full of His peace and joy.

Chapter 12

FREQUENTLY ASKED QUESTIONS

WITH A MINISTRY as supernatural as deliverance, there is no shortage of questions. The truth is that the supernatural realm is incredibly complex and deep. I feel that the more experience I get and the more I learn about deliverance, the more questions I have. At times it feels as if there are more questions than answers. In the Gospels it was normal for the disciples to ask Jesus questions, to which He often responded with a parable, or a story. My point is that it's normal to have questions, especially when doing deliverance ministry.

I host a live-stream show where people can call in and ask questions. It's not only for deliverance questions, but about 80 percent of the questions are related to deliverance. I currently have over one hundred hours of video answering questions on my YouTube channel, so I'm no stranger to all the questions people have as they begin to cast out demons. My goal is to answer any questions I might have missed through the duration of this book and hopefully cover any you may have also. This is not an exhaustive list but simply the most frequently asked questions I get repeatedly.

Question 1: Can I cast demons out of myself?

Let me begin by affirming that all things are possible in Christ. I never want to dismiss the potential for something to occur, as God can accomplish anything He desires. However, it's important to note that self-deliverance is not a biblical method for casting out demons. The biblical model we observe is believers actively going out and casting out demons. This isn't to say self-deliverance never occurred or that it's inherently unscriptural. I would suggest considering self-deliverance only after you've already undergone deliverance with someone else, to maintain your deliverance, but not as the initial method to seek freedom. Several challenges are associated with self-deliverance, which is why I don't recommend it unless it's your only option.

The first challenge is that the demons may begin to manifest, so you cannot speak out. This might be when you're trying to renounce or deal with unforgiveness, and they may speak out of you. It's very hard to command a demon to leave you when it's currently trying to speak out of you. You may also have a hard time discerning what demons are there because you might think it's just your thoughts.

Another challenge is that nobody will be there to pray you through. James 5:16 says, "Confess your sins to each other and pray for each other so that you may be healed. The earnest prayer of a righteous person has great power and produces wonderful results." There is supernatural power when someone prays for you that you will not have when trying to do self-deliverance. If you're willing to overcome these challenges and there is nobody to pray for deliverance in your proximity, following are a few helpful tips for performing self-deliverance.

Do it the same way you do regular deliverance. I would suggest going through the same seven-step process I taught in chapter 7. Start with renouncing things, dealing with unforgiveness, and verbally telling the demons to leave you. When you feel a demon coming up and about to leave, take a deep breath or expel your breath. Remember, the same word for breath or wind is *spirit*. Many spirits leave through exhaling, coughing, or yawning. This might sound weird, but I suggest doing this in front of a mirror so you can confront the demon. Do your best to be aggressive, and let it know that you know it is there and it must leave in Jesus' name. Here is a prayer you can say standing in front of a mirror:

> *Lord, I come before You today asking for complete and total deliverance. I know this is part of the finished work of the cross, and I receive my inheritance. Satan, you have no power over me; I am not your home, and you must leave me today. I bind and cast out every unclean spirit that is living inside me, known or unknown. I command you to leave in the name of Jesus Christ. You must go into the abyss and never return. I break every generational curse, word curse, and legal right that remains. I cancel every contract, assignment, and plan of Satan by the blood of Jesus, and in the name of Jesus, every unclean spirit must go now! God, I pray that You will fill me with Your Holy Spirit right now in Jesus' name. Amen.*

Question 2: Can someone who has demons when they die still go to heaven?

I want to make something very clear: The presence of a demon cannot prevent you from being saved. As I said before, many Christians live their entire lives demonized, not realizing they can be set free. There will be millions who have died and will die in the future who were Christians their entire lives but never had deliverance available to them, so they ended up dying with demons still in them. The basis of your salvation is not determined by whether you have a demon. It's determined by what Jesus did on the cross. The simplest way to put it is that those who have a relationship with Christ can be sure they are saved. Having a relationship with Christ produces a changed lifestyle.

First John 2:29 says, "Since we know that Christ is righteous, we also know that all who do what is right are God's children." John is saying we know Christ is righteous because He lived a righteous life, and the telltale sign that you're His children is that you live a righteous life. This is one of the true marks of a genuine Christian: a changed lifestyle. In John 14:15 Jesus says, "If you love me, obey my commandments." When you experience God's love, you reciprocate it and obey what He says. Second Corinthians 13:5–6 (ESV) says,

> Examine yourselves, to see whether you are in the faith. Test yourselves. Or do you not realize this about yourselves, that Jesus Christ is in you?—unless indeed you fail to meet the test! I hope you will find out that we have not failed the test.

So there should be evidence of a changed life to determine whether we truly are in the faith. Sadly, many self-proclaiming Christians are not true born-again conversions; in that case, those people will not inherit the kingdom of God. Only those with a genuine relationship with Christ will be saved.

It is possible to have demons and not give in to the urges or desires they feed you. It's just much harder to live a Christian life. Demons can't make you sin, but they can give you intense desires to sin; they can give you dominating thoughts and distract you from your destiny. Deliverance does give incredible relief from these demonic forces, but let me be clear: You can be truly saved and have demons simultaneously. So if you die as a Christian with demons, your soul and spirit will be with God, and the demons you had on this earth will likely wander, looking for a new body and a new assignment. This is why I believe people say graveyards and hospitals have increased demonic activity, as the demons of the deceased are looking for new victims.

Your salvation is not determined by whether you have a demon. It's determined by what Jesus did on the cross.

So can a Christian who lived their whole life with demons die and go to heaven? Yes, they can if they had a relationship with Jesus, followed His commands, and put their faith in the finished work of the cross.

Question 3: Isn't it dangerous to cast out demons in a public setting? Won't the demons jump out of one person into another?

This question is one of the main reasons deliverances rarely happen in the modern church. Many people have the false idea that if you cast a demon out, it will jump into the other people in the room. This is completely unscriptural. Nowhere in Scripture do we find the Bible warning us of demons jumping out of one person into another person. In fact, if we look at the deliverance ministry of Jesus, we find Him constantly casting out demons in public. Looking at Acts 8, we see Philip the evangelist casting out demons in a public setting. This idea that deliverance must be done in private is often repeated in the body of Christ and is a fear tactic of the devil to keep deliverance from taking place.

The devil *hates* deliverance and will create every lie possible to prevent this ministry from happening.

I also want you to consider where we command the demons to go when we cast them out. We are telling them to go into the abyss, which means they cannot jump into someone else. We are taking them out of circulation. If you took a counterfeit hundred-dollar bill to the bank, they would destroy it and not put it back into circulation. In deliverance, by commanding the demons to go to the abyss, as discussed in a previous chapter, we are not giving them the ability to jump into someone else. Satan and his kingdom are the only ones in danger during a deliverance.

Now, some might say, "But Isaiah, after a deliverance session, my friend who was there started having a bunch of manifestations. I think the demon jumped into them!" To that I would say, "Likely your friend being around a deliverance triggered the demons they already had." It's very common for someone with demons who is around a deliverance to have their demons manifest themselves. I can only speculate that maybe it's because the demon is now exposed and doesn't have to try to hide anymore, or maybe the demon is just scared, causing it to manifest. Regardless, this is a common phenomenon. Let's not be concerned with demons jumping from one person to another person and instead do what the Bible says to do and cast them out.

Question 4: Can deliverance happen if the demon doesn't manifest at all?

I will be the first to admit that when there is a dramatic manifestation during a deliverance, such as someone growling, slithering like a snake on the ground, or speaking in demonic tongues, it often feels as though the deliverance is more effective. But this is not true; the goal of a deliverance is not a dramatic manifestation. It's the person being set free from the demonic spirit. If you look at the story in Luke 13 of the woman who for eighteen years was bent over because of a spirit of infirmity, we do not see any dramatic manifestation, yet she is set free from her bondage. Although manifestations are common when doing deliverance, they are not required for true freedom.

Years ago I was praying for a young man who was heavily demonized. We started with the usual renouncing and dealing with unforgiveness and then moved into confronting the demon. We spent at least two hours calling out every demon we could think of, pleading for the blood of Jesus, and playing worship music. I mean, we tried everything to get a demon to manifest. We knew demons were there, as he had dealt with constant manifestations before. After two hours I had exhausted every method I knew of and just felt at peace. I could tell he was discouraged because he was expecting something dramatic to happen. I was a bit discouraged as well but felt in my spirit that he was set free. I told him, "Let's give it a week. Contact me to let me know how you're feeling and if the symptoms you were dealing with before have changed."

The next day, he called me, saying everything was gone. He woke up feeling lighter and refreshed, and all the demonic voices and desires were gone. He boldly said, "Wow, I'm free! I have never felt this way before." I kept checking in on him every few months, and to this day he is walking in freedom. He did not have any manifestations during

> The devil *hates* deliverance and will create every lie possible to prevent this ministry from happening.

his deliverance, but what he did have was much better, and that was complete freedom in Jesus' name.

Question 5: Are spiritual spouses a real thing?

Spiritual spouse is a term rarely used in America, but in many parts of the world it is understood to be when a demonic spirit claims you as their husband or wife by either consent or nonconsent. It often will fight and cause division between you and any human being who attempts to love you or build a relationship with you. These spirits wreak havoc in relationships and marriages. They violate the laws of God because God never intended for people to marry spirits. Let me show you this in Scripture.

Genesis 6:1–5 says,

> Then the people began to multiply on the earth, and daughters were born to them. The sons of God saw the beautiful women and took any they wanted as their wives. Then the LORD said, "My Spirit will not put up with humans for such a long time, for they are only mortal flesh. In the future, their normal lifespan will be no more than 120 years." In those days, and for some time after, giant Nephilites lived on the earth, for whenever the sons of God had intercourse with women, they gave birth to children who became the heroes and famous warriors of ancient times. The LORD observed the extent of human wickedness on the earth, and he saw that everything they thought or imagined was consistently and totally evil.

In this biblical account, fallen angels were marrying humans and having sex with them, producing an offspring called the Nephilim. I don't want to open a can of worms and go into the Nephilim, but I wanted to show you that even back then, fallen angels were taking humans as their wives.

From my experience, there are a few sins that open the door to spiritual spouses—that is, demons who think they're married to you. To name a few, fornication, pornography, masturbation, engaging in spiritism or channeling, adultery, ritual work, and all forms of witchcraft and divination. I would deal with casting out a spiritual spouse in the same way I deal with any other demon. Nothing special needs to be done other than knowing they are real.

Question 6: Is it common for the same person to have multiple deliverances?

This is a very common question that needs to be addressed because many pastors and leaders shame people for going through deliverance more than once. If you go to the doctor because you have pain in your body, and he prescribes you something and you feel better; then six months go by, and you're sick again, and you go back to the same doctor, he is not going to shame you and say, "You were just here six months ago! Why are you back?" A doctor will see you over and over as long as you need help. If a secular doctor will do that, why is it that pastors shame people for coming for continual help? I don't think we should make a habit of constantly going through deliverance, but if there is still a demon, I don't care if it takes ten sessions, let's get the person free. Here are a few reasons you might need multiple deliverances:

- The person being delivered was not ready and must return when they are. It's common that during the first deliverance session someone goes through, they are not fully ready to be free. There may be fear, unbelief, or even confusion, especially if it's their first time receiving deliverance. I have had multiple occasions where I could tell someone wasn't ready and told them, "Hey, how about you do a two-to-three-day fast and come back when you're ready." They agreed, did the fast, and came back and got fully free.

- There were hidden demons that were not revealed in previous sessions. It is very common for demons to remain hidden throughout an entire deliverance session. If the deliverance minister wasn't thorough or the demon just outsmarted them, they will likely need another session to deal with that demon.

- You ran out of time. Deliverances can be really long. Schedules don't always permit you to go for three or four hours, if needed, so there may be situations where you need to stop and decide you need to do another session.

- The last and most common reason someone might need multiple deliverances is if they received altar deliverance for five to ten minutes and need a more thorough session. I discussed in a previous chapter how altar deliverances are powerful but not always the most effective due to time constraints. Sometimes it's a great place to start, but personal deliverance is usually what's needed to finish the job. No matter the reason, if someone needs multiple deliverance sessions, let's not shame them. Instead, let's take the time to help them until they are fully free.

Question 7: Can a person who has demons minister deliverance?

The answer is yes; the presence of a demon in you does not take away your authority in Christ. We are not exercising our power or our authority when doing deliverance. We are exercising Christ's authority and power. Deliverance is not about what we have or what we have done. It's about the finished work of Christ. In the same way someone who is sick in their body can lay hands on and pray for the sick, someone who is demonized can effectively minister deliverance.

However, if you're demonized, I would highly recommend getting deliverance yourself before doing deliverance on others. The reason is that the demons in you can hinder and interrupt the deliverance you're trying to do on someone else. Some people do many deliverances before they even realize they themselves need freedom. At the end of the day seek deliverance if you need it, but don't sit around waiting until you're completely free (in your eyes) before you start praying for others.

Question 8: My church doesn't practice deliverance ministry. Should I leave?

This is a very touchy subject, as I would hate to be the reason that someone decides to leave their church. But let me give you my honest opinion. Deliverance is not a salvation issue; it is a secondary issue of whether someone believes in it. It is possible to attend a good church that does not teach on deliverance and get teaching on it elsewhere. However, personally, I would never attend a church that does not believe in and practice the ministry of deliverance. The reason is that if I can't bring my demonized friends and family to my own church to receive freedom, where can I take them? The church should be a healthy place where people can come and receive healing and freedom. It's sad how many pastors don't practice deliverance and how many churches deny the need for it. I have pinpointed a few reasons that a pastor or church might not actively participate in deliverance ministry.

1. They are ignorant and have never experienced it. This might sound harsh, but to be ignorant means they don't know. This is a very poor excuse, considering Jesus cast out demons everywhere He went. Our pastors must pursue this knowledge

and be good shepherds who fight for their flocks. If you don't know, then learn, buy books, watch YouTube teachings, and study the Gospel accounts. You can do plenty of things to learn about the topic.

2. They are lazy. Sadly, many lazy pastors would rather spend their days golfing than casting out demons. Casting out demons takes an extreme amount of time and energy and usually goes without any physical reward. You must sacrifice time and energy to see the captives get free.

3. They are preaching a partial gospel, and this is the part they leave out. In modern Christianity people basically pick and choose what parts of the Bible they want to obey; they treat it like a buffet. Some churches don't like holiness, so they leave it out completely; some churches don't like talking about repentance or hell, so you never hear about it; some churches don't believe that miraculous healing and deliverance are for today, so they leave it out completely. In Romans 15:19 the apostle Paul says, "…by the power of signs and wonders, through the power of the Spirit of God. So from Jerusalem all the way around to Illyricum, I have fully proclaimed the gospel of Christ."

Notice he says "by the power of signs and wonders…I have fully proclaimed the gospel of Christ." A gospel without the miraculous signs and wonders is a partial gospel. In summary, I personally would not attend a church that does not believe in and regularly practice healing and deliverance, but if I were you, I would pray and ask the Lord to speak to you about this.

Question 9: I need deliverance, but there is no church or Christian around me that offers it. What should I do?

I got this question in my call-in show every week for months, so I decided to do something about it. The sad reality is that we have churches on every corner, yet very few are praying for people to be set free from demonic bondage. Frustrated by this question, I asked God, "What can I do to help all those who are in bondage with nobody to pray for them?" That's when He gave me the vision for the deliverance map. I knew I had been training people online for months on deliverance, so how could I connect the people being trained with those needing freedom?

> A gospel without the miraculous signs and wonders is a partial gospel.

With the help of a small tech start-up, we created an interactive map where people who need deliverance can connect with people who are currently equipped to do deliverance. Once connected, they can then meet at a neutral location and get prayer. To be on the map, you must submit an application and do a short video call. Once approved, a pin goes onto our interactive map, and instantly people can start reaching out to you based on location for prayer. I didn't realize how this would take off.

We now have over two thousand people on the map doing deliverances, fifty thousand webpage visits a week, and literally thousands of testimonies of people receiving freedom. This entire vision is about empowering the body of Christ to do the work that Jesus did. To access the map, go to www.Deliverancemap.com or www.Isaiahsaldivar.com/deliverance. From there you look around your area at the ministers we have listed, and reach out for prayer. It's as simple as that. We add and take people off daily based on applications and complaints that come in, so it's a dynamic map that is always changing. There is no doubt that God has been raising up an army in the last days.

Question 10: Can children have demons? Do you do deliverance on them differently?

Children having demons is a biblical reality. Jesus did deliverance on children; in fact, of the seven deliverances the Gospels tell us about, two were with children. The first account is in Luke 9:37, where a boy's father first brought his demonized son to Jesus' disciples, but they were unable to deliver the boy. Jesus came down from the Mount of Transfiguration and ultimately delivered the boy, and when the disciples asked why they couldn't, He said this type (speaking of the spirit) only comes out through prayer and fasting. The second account is the Syrophoenician woman in Matthew 15:22, who came to Jesus begging Him to deliver her daughter. After a dialogue with the woman, He said to her, "Your faith is great. It shall be done," and her daughter was delivered at once.

Both these parents had no problem identifying that the source of their kids' troubles was demons. Many parents today would never even consider that their children could be demonized, but these parents recognized it. In America people have a hard time. In other countries there is not a struggle about this issue. They understand the concept. Children are actually more vulnerable to demons than adults, and that's because they are dependent on their parents to be their spiritual guardians and protectors.

As parents we often fail to protect our kids from demons. The Bible says in Proverbs 22:15, "Foolishness is bound up in the heart of a child; the rod of discipline will remove it far from him." Many parents don't even believe in discipline anymore. Most parents are more concerned with being their kids' friends than spiritual guardians, but understand that God has called you to guard them. They are being assaulted with all types of demonic influences everywhere.

The second thing we learn from Jesus is that the presence

of demons in our kids can be revealed by what is happening to them. The boy's father said in Luke 9:39, "A spirit seizes him, and he suddenly screams; it throws him into convulsions so that he foams at the mouth. It scarcely ever leaves him and is destroying him." Mark 9:17 says, "Teacher, I brought my son so you could heal him. He is possessed by an evil spirit that won't let him talk. And whenever this spirit seizes him, it throws him violently to the ground. Then he foams at the mouth, grinds his teeth, and becomes rigid." In Mark 9:21 he said, "Since he was a little boy, the spirit often throws him into the fire or into water, trying to kill him." These were symptoms of the boy having a demon.

Most parents today would go straight to a medical doctor, but this man went straight to Jesus, understanding that a doctor can't help if there is a demon. In Matthew 15:22 the Syrophoenician woman said, "My daughter is grievously vexed by a demon." This means to be harassed, so she was saying this demon was seriously harassing her daughter. So we see that the parents knew by how their kids acted. There were visible indicators in their children's behavior.

The third thing Jesus teaches us is that the parents need to take initiative. In both stories the parent took the initiative. You can't wait until your kid tells you, "Mommy, I need help." If you see your kid is demonized, take the initiative. A child can't go to our deliverance map and set up a deliverance, so this is where the parents step in.

The fourth thing Jesus teaches us is that He honors the parents' faith in both stories. The boy's father first went to the disciples, and when he saw they were unable to help, he pressed through to get to Jesus. Don't get discouraged or disappointed if it takes some time to find help. Even though the disciples wanted to silence her, the woman was persistent in her faith. You need to be willing to do what you need to do to get your kid delivered.

I have a few recommendations before your child gets deliverance. First, you should get delivered; if deliverance is good enough for them, it should be good enough for you. You should lead the way by going through a deliverance before they do. Demons attached to your bloodline may get released at your deliverance. It is not required that you do this before they get deliverance, but it is highly recommended.

Another recommendation is that when you do their deliverance, you do not need to go through all the unforgiveness and renouncing. I would keep it simple and start commanding the demons to leave. Frank and Ida MaebHammond have an amazing book called *A Manual for Children's Deliverance*. They discuss how to deal with each age. Here is an excerpt for reference. For ages three to six, this is how Hammond would explain the deliverance before he started:

> "Jane, God says that your body is like a temple, a special house where His Holy Spirit lives. But bad spirits call your body 'their house.' The Bible says that when a demon is put out of a person, he is put out of his 'house.'
>
> "So, your body is a house where evil spirits want to live. Now, if you are in a house and you want to come out, how do you get out?" We then point to her mouth. "Through the door. Where is the door? Your mouth is the door. When I say, 'Demon, you come out of Jane,' it will come out through your mouth." Jane is then instructed to open her mouth and blow out some breath. This initiates an act of her will. "Now, a demon is a breath, so let us see you blow your breath out." (We show her what we mean by letting our own breath out and blowing through the mouth).
>
> "Another way you can get him out is to cough him out." (We then practice coughing). "That is how demons will come out through your mouth. Your body is God's house, and your mouth is the door to the house. How else can a demon come out of you? A house has windows. Your eyes are the windows of your

house. Have you ever seen someone climb out of a window? If a demon comes out of you through your eyes, through your windows, you may have tears. So, if you cry and shed tears, you will know that a demon is coming out of you through your windows."

Then we tell Jane, "There are two kinds of spirits in the world. Do you know what God's Spirit is called? He is called the Holy Spirit. The devil has lots of spirits. He is not as powerful as God. He is not everywhere like God, so he has to have many spirits to help him, and these are called demon spirits. Now, Jane, we are going to command the bad spirits to come out of you. When we tell them to go, you can help them to leave by breathing them out."[1]

CONCLUSION

A
S YOU CONCLUDE this journey through understanding and engaging in the ministry of deliverance, it's essential not only to absorb the knowledge you've gained but to step out in faith and put it into action. Jesus' words in Mark 16:17, "And these signs will accompany those who believe: In my name, they will drive out demons," serve as a powerful reminder that this ministry is not just for a select few but for all believers who walk in faith and authority.

Each chapter of this book has equipped you with biblical insights and practical steps—whether it's recognizing the presence of demons, understanding how they gain entry, or mastering the process of casting them out. Now it's your turn to step into this calling with confidence and boldness.

Do not allow fear, doubt, or inaction to hinder you from exercising the authority given to you by Christ. The knowledge you've gained about how Jesus cast out demons, the signs of demonic presence, and the importance of maintaining your deliverance is meant to empower you to help others experience freedom. Remember, it's not about your strength but the power of Jesus' name and the victory He has already won. As you go forward, be vigilant, stay rooted in prayer, and rely on the Holy Spirit to guide you. The mission of deliverance is urgent and necessary, and you are now equipped to be a vessel of God's power and deliverance in the lives of others. A hurting, broken world is waiting for you; your time is now!

NOTES

Chapter 1

1. Derek Prince, "Defense Against Discouragement," Derek Prince Ministries, accessed July 10, 2024, https://www.derekprince.com/teaching/12-11.
2. Don Stewart, "Were the Sons of God Fallen Angels?," Blue Letter Bible, accessed May 30, 2024, https://www.blueletterbible.org/faq/don_stewart/don_stewart_724.cfm.

Chapter 3

1. Don Dickerman, *When Pigs Move In: How to Sweep Clean the Demonic Influences Impacting Your Life and the Lives of Others* (Charisma House, 2009), 21.
2. Sam Storms, "Can a Christian Be Demonized? Part One," Sam Storms, February 16, 2017, https://www.samstorms.org/enjoying-god-blog/post/can-a-christian-be-demonized-part-one.
3. Storms, "Can a Christian Be Demonized?"
4. John Eckhardt, "Can a Christian Have a Demon?," *Charisma*, August 22, 2015, https://mycharisma.com/charisma-archive/john-eckhardt-can-a-christian-have-a-demon/.

Chapter 4

1. "Children and Teens: Statistics," RAINN, accessed May 20, 2024, https://www.rainn.org/statistics/children-and-teens.

2. Oxford Languages, s.v. "trauma," accessed July 10, 2024, https://www.google.com/search?q=trauma+definition&rlz=1C1GCEU_enUS966US966&oq=trauma.

3. "How Should a Christian View Yoga?," Got Questions, accessed June 28, 2024, https://www.gotquestions.org/Christian-yoga.html.

4. "Yoga Mudras," Yoga Journal, accessed May 20, 2024, https://www.yogajournal.com/practice/energetics/mudra/.

Chapter 5

1. Oxford Languages, s.v. "camouflage," accessed May 31, 2024, https://www.google.com/search?q=camouflage+definition&rlz=1C1GCEU_enUS966US966&oq=camouflage.

2. "Schizophrenia," National Institute of Mental Health, accessed June 4, 2024, https://www.nimh.nih.gov/health/topics/schizophrenia#:~:text=Psychotic%20symptoms%20include%3A,or%20friends%20notice%20a%20problem.

Chapter 6

1. Bible Study Tools, s.v. "*Shamar*," accessed May 22, 2024, https://www.biblestudytools.com/lexicons/hebrew/nas/shamar.html.

2. Lexie Pelchen, "Surprising Home Burglary Facts and Stats," Forbes Home, April 30, 2024, https://www.forbes.com/home-improvement/home-security/home-invasion-statistics/.

3. *Merriam-Webster*, s.v. "poltergeist," accessed August 16, 2024, https://www.merriam-webster.com/dictionary/poltergeist#:~:text=Etymology,words%20from%20the%20same%20year.

4. Bible Study Tools, s.v. *"cherum,"* accessed July 12, 2024, https://www.biblestudytools.com/lexicons/hebrew/nas/ cherem.html.

5. "What Does the Bible Say About Crystals?" Bibleinfo. com, accessed May 22, 2024, https://www.bibleinfo. com/en/questions/what-does-bible-say-about-crystals.

6. "Ouija," Wikipedia, accessed May 23, 2024, https:// en.wikipedia.org/wiki/Ouija.

7. "Dream Catchers: Where Do They Come From and How to Use Them?" *Harpo,* accessed May 23, 2024, https://www.harpo-paris.com/en/blog/post/10-les-attrape-reves-quelle-histoire-et-comment-les-utiliser-.

8. Brett Larkin, "What Is a Dream Catcher and What Does It Do?" Tiny Rituals, July 24, 2022, https:// tinyrituals.co/blogs/tiny-rituals/dream-catcher-meaning.

9. Blue Letter Bible, s.v. *"pesel,"* accessed May 23, 2024, https://www.blueletterbible.org/lexicon/h6459/kjv/ wlc/0-1/.

10. *Merriam-Webster,* s.v. "venerate," accessed July 10, 2024, https://www.merriam-webster.com/dictionary/venerate; *Merriam-Webster,* s.v. "worship," accessed July 10, 2024, https://www.merriam-webster.com/dictionary/worship.

11. "10 Benefits of Burning Sage, How to Get Started, and More," Healthline, accessed May 24, 2024, https://www. healthline.com/health/benefits-of-burning-sage.

12. "Burning Sage: Everything to Know About This Ancient Ritual," Beauty Daily, accessed May 24, 2024, https:// beautydaily.clarins.co.uk/wellness/mindfulness/burning-sage.

CHAPTER 9

1. *Merriam-Webster,* s.v. "resist," accessed July 12, 2024, https://www.merriam-webster.com/dictionary/resist.

CHAPTER 11

1. Blue Letter Bible, s.v. *"holoteles,"* accessed June 19, 2024, https://www.blueletterbible.org/lexicon/g3651/kjv/tr/0-1/.
2. "Pornography Statistics," Covenant Eyes, accessed June 28, 2024, https://www.covenanteyes.com/pornstats/;_ Anna Pawlikowska-Gorzelańczyk et al., "Impact of Internet Addiction, Social Media Use and Online Pornography on the Male Sexual Function in Times of the COVID-19 Pandemic," *Journal of Clinical Medicine* 12, no. 19 (October 8, 2023): 6407, https://doi.org/10.3390/jcm12196407.
3. "What Are the Greek and Hebrew Words for 'Confess'?," Bible.org, accessed July 14, 2024, https://bible.org/question/what-are-greek-and-hebrew-words-"confess".
4. Bible Tools, s.v. *"tsuwm,"* accessed June 19, 2024, https://www.bibletools.org/index.cfm/fuseaction/Lexicon.show/ID/H6684/tsuwm.htm.
5. Bible Hub, s.v. *"alēthēs,"* accessed June 19, 2024, https://biblehub.com/greek/227.htm.
6. "Free From Bondage and Worry," Kingdom Winds, June 20, 2023, https://kingdomwinds.com/free-from-bondage-and-worry.

CHAPTER 12

1. Frank and Ida Mae Hammond, *A Manual for Children's Deliverance* (Impact Christian Books, 2010), 46–47.

ABOUT THE AUTHOR

ALTHOUGH RAISED IN the church, Isaiah Saldivar turned his back on God as a teenager and wanted nothing more to do with Christianity. But God had other plans. On January 12, 2011, he attended a church service in Modesto, California, out of obligation—not realizing that when he sat in what seemed like "just another church pew," his life was about to change forever.

After the preacher taught a Spirit-filled message about changing the world in the name of Jesus, Isaiah knew he couldn't possibly stay in his seat any longer. By the end of the service he ran to the altar and prayed a simple prayer that would change his entire life. He said, "God, if You're real, I'll give You everything." In an audible voice, Isaiah heard God clearly tell him, "I am going to use you to preach the gospel to every nation."

Undone and deeply repentant, Isaiah disposed of every reminder and item that encompassed a part of his previous life.

Overwhelmed by God's tangible presence, he sought counsel from his uncle Ben Lucero (Nino), who was a minister.

After mentorship Ben asked Isaiah, "What do you want to do next?" Isaiah knew he had been shown a vivid vision of people praying at his house. Thus the mandate was simple. He replied, "We need to pray, and people will gather." With the help of his uncle Ben, Isaiah did what God had told him to do—he and five others started praying together at his house. As a result, people began to gather and gather and gather. Soon enough, signs, wonders, and miracles broke out as God's power was made perfect on the small but growing prayer team.

Numbering more than four hundred people every week, the prayer meeting (now known as The Awakening 209) quickly outgrew Isaiah's modest ranch home. What began as a handful of ordinary people desperate to see an extraordinary God move in power and truth became a global revival that went from 2011 to 2019.

Isaiah has spoken at more than five hundred churches, conferences, and other events. He travels and preaches a message of revival and repentance. His focus for the past several years has been reaching people through social media, and today his ministry reaches up to eight million people per week. He hosts a weekly podcast called *Revival Lifestyle* that is in the top 1 percent of podcasts in the world. He also uploads videos every day to his YouTube channel, which currently has nine hundred thousand subscribers.

Isaiah and his wife, Alyssa, have four daughters: Justice, Journey, Harvest, and Nova. He and his family reside in central California and attend The House Modesto church.